B40

PERSPECTIVES

A Multicultural Portrait of
The Move West

By Petra Press

Marshall Cavendish

New York • London • Toronto

Cover: While the introduction of epidemic diseases to North America had devastating consequences, another significant Spanish import, the horse, opened up tremendous opportunities for American Indians, particularly for hunting buffalo.

Published by
Marshall Cavendish Corporation
2415 Jerusalem Avenue
P.O. Box 587
North Bellmore, New York 11710, USA

Project director: Mark Sachner
Art director: Sabine Beaupré
Picture researcher: Diane Laska
Indexer: Valerie Weber
Marshall Cavendish development editor: MaryLee Knowlton
Marshall Cavendish editorial director: Evelyn Fazio

Editorial consultants: Mark S. Guardalabene, Milwaukee Public Schools; Yolanda Ayubi, Ph.D., Consultant on Ethnic Issues, U.S. Department of Labor

Picture Credits: Sabine Beaupré, 1993: 8 (bottom); © The Bettmann Archive: Cover, 8 (top), 9, 10 (top), 12, 13, 14, 15, 18, 19, 20, 21 (bottom), 23, 24, 25, 26, 30, 32, 37, 38, 40, 41, 42, 44, 49, 52, 53, 55, 56, 57, 58, 59, 60, 61, 62, 64, 65, 66, 70, 72, 75 (both); © Culver Pictures: 47 (bottom); © Charles Phelps Cushing/H. Armstrong Roberts: 16, 35, 74 (top); © H. Armstrong Roberts: 10 (bottom), 11, 21 (top), 28-29, 47 (top), 68; © UPI/Bettmann: 6, 74 (bottom)

Library of Congress Cataloging-in-Publication Data

Press, Petra.
        A multicultural portrait of the move West / Petra Press.
            p.   cm. — (Perspectives)
        Includes bibliographical references and index.
        Summary: Describes the history of westward expansion from the point of view of minorities and women.
        ISBN 1-85435-658-5 :
        1. West (U.S.)—History—Juvenile literature. 2. Indians of North America—West (U.S.)—History—Juvenile literature. 3. Pluralism (Social sciences)—West (U.S.)—History—Juvenile literature. 4. United States—Territorial expansion—Juvenile literature. 5. West (U.S.)—Discovery and exploration—Juvenile literature. 6. Frontier and pioneer life—West (U.S.)—Juvenile literature. [1. West (U.S.)—History. 2. Indians of North America—History. 3. Frontier and pioneer life. 4. Minorities.] I. Title. II. Series: Perspectives (Marshall Cavendish Corporation)
F591.P915   1993
978—dc20   93-10317
                                                                                                                  CIP
                                                                                                                  AC

To Opa – PP

To PS – MS

CONTENTS

About *Perspectives*

Perspectives is a series of multicultural portraits of events and topics in U.S. history. Each volume examines these events and topics not only from the perspective of the white European-Americans who make up the majority of the U.S. population, but also from that of the nation's many people of color and other ethnic minorities, such as African-Americans, Asian-Americans, Hispanic-Americans, and American Indians. These people, along with women, have been given little attention in traditional accounts of U.S. history. And yet their impact on historical events has been great.

The terms *American Indian*, *Hispanic-American*, *Anglo-American*, *Black*, *African-American*, and *Asian-American*, like *European-American* and *white*, are used by the authors in this series to identify people of various national origins. Labeling people is a serious business, and what we call a group depends on many things. For example, a few decades ago it was considered acceptable to use the words *colored* or *Negro* to label people of African origin. Today, these words are outdated and often a sign of ignorance or outright prejudice. Some people even consider *Black* less acceptable than *African-American* because it focuses on a person's skin color rather than national origins. And yet *Black* has many practical uses, particularly to describe people whose origins are not only African but Caribbean or Latin American as well.

If we must label people, it's better to be as specific as possible. That is a goal of *Perspectives* — to be as precise and fair as possible in the labeling of people by race, ethnicity, national origin, or other factors, such as gender or disability. When necessary and possible, Americans of Mexican origin will be called *Mexican-Americans*. Americans of Irish origin will be called *Irish-Americans*, and so on. The same goes for American Indians: when possible, specific Indians are identified by their tribal names, such as the *Chippewa* or *Mohawk*. But in a discussion of various Indian groups, tribal origins may not always be entirely clear, and so it may be more practical to use *American Indian*, a term that has widespread use among Indians and non-Indians alike.

Even within a group, individuals may disagree over the labels they prefer for their group: *Black* or *African-American*? *Hispanic* or *Latino*? *American Indian* or *native American*? *White*, *Anglo*, or *European-American*? Different situations often call for different labels. The labels used in *Perspectives* represent an attempt to be fair, accurate, and perhaps most importantly, to be mindful of what people choose to call *themselves*.

A Note About *The Move West*

To many people, the American West means John Wayne riding tall in the saddle in cowboy boots and Stetson hat, his face weather-beaten from riding the range. He's the all-American hero, ready to take the law into his own hands to make sure Good triumphs over Evil. Other people might think of covered wagons and feisty, Protestant pioneers braving the Overland Trail. But contrary to the Anglo-American legends perpetuated by Hollywood, these were not the only (or even the most typical) western settlers. African-Americans, Asians, Hispanics, in fact immigrants from all over the world, played an important part in creating western communities, and there are at least as many versions of western history as there were people to settle it.

The history of the American West does not begin with Anglo explorers like Lewis and Clark, or even with the Spanish *conquistadors* who conquered parts of the Southwest. Europeans called it a "frontier of civilization" waiting to be settled, but the American West wasn't really settled so much as it was conquered, and the costs were staggering in a number of different ways. Because American Indians didn't share the European lust for land and power or their Christian religious beliefs, the first white explorers and traders labeled them savages.

For the Indians of the American West, the relatively small part of their history that includes other cultures has meant horrific loss, not just of life, but of homeland and cultural identity. There was also the 150 years of ecological damage to wildlife and natural resources with mindless waste and pollution, as well as the political and sociological effects of the deep-seated animosity that developed between diverse cultural groups. We're still paying the costs of western expansion today.

How did the Indians interact with traders, missionaries, settlers, and soldiers? What opportunities did the West offer an ex-slave from Alabama, an Irish-Catholic fleeing her homeland's potato famine, or an Indian child growing up on a reservation?

How was life in a Protestant farming community different from cow-punching or prospecting for gold? What part did Chinese immigrants play in building the West? One in every three cowboys was either Black or Hispanic; what kind of discrimination did they face? These are some of the questions we address in this book.

This is not a shoot-'em-up history of virtuous cowboys and cutthroat Indians. It's an attempt to describe the West and the people who settled it as they really were, good and bad. Although it may not always present a flattering picture of the American character, it does show how the real West helped shape the way we see ourselves today and the way we act, both as individuals and as a nation. The real story of the American West is even more remarkable than the legends.

A Kiowa Indian woman and child.

A Multicultural Portrait of the Move West

CHAPTER ONE

The First Western Americans

The books and movies of the last 150 years invented a Wild West that never really existed — but one in which almost everyone believes. In movies like *How The West Was Won*, life on the American frontier was colorful and exciting. For the average white cowboy, branding steer, outwitting savage Indians, and joining the marshal's posse to hunt down outlaws were all part of a normal day's work.

The Wild West of myth and legend is made up of stereotypes, not of real people. In popular stories, outlaws like Jesse James and Billy the Kid were colorful and heroic. The cowboys who tamed the rough frontier were all as tough and handsome as a young John Wayne. Dance hall girls all had hearts of gold, and the only good Indian was a dead Indian.

Authors and directors exaggerated historical events such as the California Gold Rush and Custer's Last Stand to create more exciting plots for their movies and books. Colorful as these stories are, the real history of this region is far more remarkable. The immigrants and American Indians who forged the history of the American West came from such an incredible mixture of ethnic, religious, and racial backgrounds that it's impossible to reduce them to just a few colorful stereotypes.

Reality vs. the Myth of the Savage Frontier

One of the most common misunderstandings about the American West is that its history began with an empty continent populated only by isolated tribes of primitive, red-skinned savages. Another misunderstanding is that European powers — and later the U.S. government — had the right to invade this territory, conquer its native inhabitants, and help themselves to its natural resources.

In reality, the history of the land expanding west from the Mississippi River over the high plains to the Pacific Coast has been evolving for thousands of years. By 1650, about the time the first Europeans started actively settling this area, there were over three hundred distinct and highly developed native cultures in North America. Some cultures had entirely disappeared by the fifteenth century, but others were growing and developing at a remarkable

Buffalo country

The Great Plains were home to both hunting tribes and to tribal farming villages. It was also buffalo country, where great herds thundered across the rolling landscape like some dark and terrible sea. To the Indians, the buffalo represented food, clothing, and lodging. The buffalo was a gift from their Creator, an animal they believed was endowed with supernatural powers. Before the arrival of the horse, Indians stalked this animal on foot, with whole lines of hunters disguised in animal skins creeping up to an unsuspecting herd. One Indian would give the signal, and they would wave and shout to stampede the buffalo over cliffs or into corrals. Sometimes they set fire to the dry prairie grasses to get the animals moving.

Native American culture areas, around 1650.

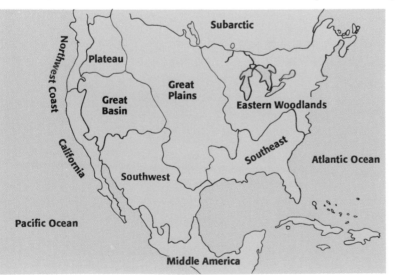

rate. The word "tribe" does not begin to describe the tremendous variety of their politics, their methods of planting, harvesting, and hunting food, the depth of their cultural patterns and spiritual beliefs, or even the size of their populations.

The Lay of the Land

As the map on this page shows, there are six major regions of native American culture in the West: the Great Plains, Southwest, Plateau, Northwest Coast, Great Basin, and California coastline regions. The Great Plains region west of the Mississippi stretches from what is now the Canadian border south to Oklahoma and Texas. The Great Plains Indians included powerful, nomadic hunters like the Blackfoot, Crow, Cheyenne, Sioux, and Comanche. But its rich and fertile farmlands were also home for the farming villages of the Pawnee, Caddo, Arikara, Wichita, and Mandan.

The desert climate of the Southwest region is harsh. Tribes that have adapted to this difficult region include the Pueblo, Hopi, Apache, Yuma, and Navajo. To the north, in the Great Basin region, the Ute, Shoshoni, and Washo cultures thrived despite the desolate sagebrush and bunch grass vegetation. On the Northwest Pacific Coast were the Chinook, Cowichan, and Yakima Indians, while the Hupa, Pomo, Chumash, and Kumja tribes could be found along the coast of California.

Each culture was unique in its religious ceremonies, social systems, and ways of adapting to its environment. Yet all shared deep spiritual beliefs based on a knowledge of, and respect for, nature. All shared social structures and governments based on such values as liberty and equality. These Indian cultures had a knowledge of herbs and other healing plants that enabled them to practice medicine. They understood geography and climate well enough to become expert farmers, trappers, and hunters. They developed sophisticated weapons and tools. And they created lasting and meaningful art.

Yet most of the non-Indian people who came west (whether they were European immigrants, Asians, or Africans) didn't see the richness of all these unique Indian cultures; they only saw "redskins." These immigrants judged Indians by the values of their own cultures. Because Indians were not Christians, they must be devil-worshippers. And because they hunted for their food and did not believe in owning land, working by a clock, or competing for material possessions, they were considered hopeless savages.

With so many unique and highly developed Indian cultures, the West of 1650 was certainly not an empty frontier. But by 1650, when the first pioneers started moving west, there were more than just Indians west of the Mississippi.

The First Europeans in the West — the Spanish

The first Europeans in the American West were neither conquerors nor explorers. They were merely lost. In 1528, a Spanish expedition left Cuba and sailed west on a mission to pillage the Mexican Gulf Coast and take slaves. Instead, the expedition was shipwrecked off the Texas coast with only four survivors, including an African slave named Estevánico and his Spanish owner. It would take these survivors eight years to get to the frontier of New Spain in Mexico, after traveling across Texas, up the Rio Grande, and into New Mexico.

The four were immediately taken as slaves by a band of wandering, starving nomadic Indians and spent several seasons like their captors, just trying to scrabble up something to eat. That usually meant bark, bugs, dung, and even old bones. When one of the Indians fell sick, the others would try to cure him with magic and herbal medicines. One day, when one of the leaders lay dying and the usual magic wasn't working, the expedition's treasurer, Alvar Núñez Cabeza de Vaca, tried praying as a last desperate effort to save him. Miraculously, the man lived and Núñez became a hero to his captors a hero with supernatural powers. Eventually, Núñez and his companions became the tribe's practicing shamans, or medicine men. Núñez was the most successful. Apparently, after a while, all four of them started believing that they really could cure the sick and bring the dead back to life.

Núñez and his three companions became so famous as shamans that they received an honorable escort on the remainder of their journey to the Spanish frontier in Mexico. Unfortunately, they had never told their Indian friends about the bands of Spanish slavers who burned and pillaged the Mexican countryside looking for men, women, and children they could carry off as slaves. It took Núñez considerable effort to keep the welcoming Spaniards from enslaving his Indian followers. But if he misled the Indians about the Spaniards, Núñez also misled the Spaniards about

Indian prophecies of disaster

One experience common to most North American Indian cultures is the prophetic dream about the white man's arrival. Many cultures, such as the Hopi in the Southwest, had myths and stories that foretold the future of humankind. These stories often predicted the arrival of a White Man who would use any means to get what he wanted. Some cultures even predicted the death and destruction this White Man brought with him, and the ultimate loss of their lands.

Alvar Núñez Cabeza de Vaca, Estevánico, and their companions.

Above: Discovery of the Missouri River is declared by Francisco Vásquez de Coronado. *Below:* Coronado's expedition crossed the prairies of the Great Southwest.

the Indians. When he talked about his journey, he relayed stories he'd heard about large and fantastically rich Indian towns just north of the area he called Nuevo Mexico.

These stories caught the imagination of Francisco Vásquez de Coronado, a Spanish conquistador. Conquistadors were Spaniards who explored and conquered new worlds for the glory of God (and their own profit) since the early 1500s. Coronado enlisted a Franciscan friar named Marcos and one of Núñez's original companions, Estevánico, to prepare the way peacefully for Coronado's expedition. Instead, Estevánico traveled ahead of the friar, going from village to village, waving his medicine rattle and demanding turquoise and women for himself.

The Zuni Indians were afraid of this strange man with black skin who was making all these demands, and they did not trust him. When Estevánico tried to tell them that a great white man had sent him ahead to arrange a peaceful meeting, the Zuni became convinced he was lying. After all, they had never seen men with white skin, either. It's possible they were afraid Estevánico was setting some sort of trap. It's also possible that some of Estevánico's Indian companions on this journey hinted to the Zunis that the Spanish — the white men — were not very friendly guests. In any case, the Zunis finally shot Estevánico as a spy.

When the news got back to the good friar, who was about a day's journey behind, he panicked and fled. Even though the friar had never made it to the city where Estevánico died, he returned to Coronado with an incredible tale about finding the fabulous Seven Cities of Cibola. Each of these cities was supposedly larger than Mexico City, with magnificent ten-story houses and architecture inlaid with turquoise and gold.

What the friar *actually* saw, in the distance, was the small Zuni *pueblo*, or village, of Hawikuh. Its two thousand people lived in modest stone and adobe houses, and the town's wealth consisted only of a supply of corn, textiles, and pottery.

Nevertheless, Friar Marcos's wonderfully inaccurate report of the Seven Cities of Cibola spread quickly and planted a vivid and appealing picture of the West in the minds of many Europeans.

The Spanish Invade New Mexico

The first of these European travelers was the Spanish conquistador Coronado, who came north on horseback with a regiment of men in 1540. The Indians of Nuevo Mexico (New Mexico) had never seen horses before, let alone white men on horseback.

Coronado considered himself to be far less cruel than other conquistadors and hoped to conquer the Pueblos peacefully. He told the Indians, who had never heard of the Catholic Pope (or of any Spanish kings, either), that the King of Spain was claiming the area because the Pope in Rome had awarded most of the hemisphere to Spain. He demanded that the Indians pay him tribute with their supplies, but some of the men from a small Tiguex pueblo refused. Coronado retaliated by burning the pueblo — and then burning the men who had resisted as an example to any other Indians who might get the same idea.

Coronado's cruelty might have caused more damage, but he left the area a year later, in 1541, disappointed that he hadn't found the fabled Seven Cities of Cibola. In the meantime he had reports of an equally fabulous imaginary kingdom north of New Mexico, on the Great Plains, that promised even greater riches.

So Coronado took his men and headed north to the Arkansas River Valley. All he found there were the grass lodges and maize fields of the Wichita Indians. He was so disappointed that he headed back to Mexico and gave up his ideas of finding any mythical cities of great wealth.

Church and State Colonize Together

For the next fifty years, other Spaniards returned to the New Mexico Pueblos to demand supplies from the Indian inhabitants. The Spanish continued using terror tactics to get what they wanted and in 1598 sent Don Juan de Onate to officially colonize the area.

De Onate announced to the Pueblos that they were now all subjects of the King of Spain, who would protect them if they submitted and severely punish them if they resisted.

The Franciscan friars announced another choice. If the Indians chose to convert to Christianity, they would go to heaven. If not, their souls were doomed to hell. Officials of both the Church and the Spanish government demanded annual payments of corn, firewood, and even Indian homes.

Many of the Pueblos resisted. In Acoma, the "Sky City," a scuffle broke out and thirteen Spaniards died.

Pope divides up New World in 1493

When Columbus returned to Spain in his flagship, the *Niña*, after establishing the first Spanish colony in the New World, Spain immediately applied to the Court of Rome for possession of these new lands. The Pope responded by decreeing that Spain was entitled to the possession of all lands discovered west of a line drawn between the North and South poles. But Portugal objected to the location of the line, so the line was redrawn in 1494. This new line gave Portugal the territory in South America that is now Brazil.

The pueblo of Acoma, New Mexico.

In retaliation, the Spaniards sacked and burned the city, killing most of the inhabitants. Only eighty men and five hundred women and children survived. The Spanish put these survivors on trial for plotting against the Spanish government. To set an example for other villages, they sentenced the men to have one foot cut off, and all the survivors to serve as slaves for twenty years.

While the Spanish conquerors at Acoma did not believe they were being unusually cruel, these atrocities did successfully curb any further uprisings among the Pueblo for the next eighty years.

The matter of Indian slavery bothered many Spanish consciences more than the mutilations, which had been a standard type of punishment throughout Europe and other cultures for centuries. In 1537, after receiving numerous petitions from Spanish missionaries living in the Western Hemisphere, the Pope in Rome officially outlawed Indian slavery in any form. It still took many more years before this was enforced in the New World, but by 1573 the Spanish were no longer even allowed to use the word *conquest* with any action involving Indians. As the approach of the Spaniards toward the Pueblo officially changed to one of pacification, an alliance between the two cultures started to develop.

An Indian medicine man, or shaman.

The Beginnings of a Spanish-Pueblo Alliance

The Spanish appointed representatives called *encomenderos* to govern the Pueblo villages. These encomenderos promised to protect the villages against Apache raiders — in return for Pueblo labor and an annual payment of corn, firewood, and other supplies. But these small villages the Spanish took as outposts were relatively weak and isolated from each other, and the Spanish came to understand that they couldn't survive and prosper without the cooperation of the Pueblos. Gradually, the lives of the Pueblo and Spanish inhabitants began to interlock, and a new social order was created.

Although the Spanish started out as the conquerors of the Pueblo people, a social system evolved that eventually gave some members of the community more status than others. This system was based on a number of factors, including a person's ancestry and ethnic background, wealth, and religion.

Because the Spanish conquerors could no longer risk alienating the Pueblos by using them as forced labor, they developed a new source for slaves. The captives that were taken in the ongoing Pueblo wars against the surrounding Apache and Navajo tribes (mostly women and children) became the slave labor force for the new Spanish-Pueblo alliance. These slaves had the least status in the community.

Buffalo run from the hunters.

Slavery, however, was only a temporary condition. After ten years, these slaves became *genizaros*, or freed slaves, and entered New Mexico society.

One step up from the genizaros on the social ladder were the people of African and Spanish descent (*mulattos*), then people of Mexican Indian and Spanish descent (*mestizos*), people of mixed African, Indian, and Spanish descent (*pardos* or *color quebrados*), followed by those of New Mexican Indian and Spanish descent (*coyotes*). Those of purely Spanish descent (*espanoles*) enjoyed the most status in this society.

The Pueblo Indians had mixed feelings about their Spanish rulers. They resented the oppressive rulership and the large tributes they had to pay each year in exchange for protection against the surrounding tribes who attacked both the Spanish and Pueblo. But the Pueblo did benefit from many of the plants and animals the Spanish introduced to the Western Hemisphere: plants such as peaches, wheat, and oats, and animals such as horses and sheep. The horse was one of two particularly significant changes the Spanish introduced; epidemic disease was the other. Both radically changed the way of life for the North American Indian.

Scientists believe that there were no epidemic diseases like smallpox, measles, whooping cough, or the plague on either the North or South American continents when Columbus landed. Because people in Europe, Asia, and Africa had been exposed to terrible epidemics over the centuries,

Good Indians vs. Bad Indians

Most Europeans saw only two kinds of Indian cultures: good Indians and bad Indians. To the white man, Indians were either harmless and childlike primitives who occasionally lent the settlers a hand with farming or exploration — or they were terrible and bloodthirsty savages who terrorized frontier settlers without warning or reason. An example of the "good Indian" stereotype is the Lone Ranger's faithful and trusty sidekick, Tonto. The nameless hoards of whooping Apaches that ambush John Wayne's wagon train are examples of "bad Indian" stereotypes.

they built up at least a partial immunity that was then passed on to their offspring. Indian populations had no immunity at all, and when an Indian village was exposed to one of these epidemics, it often lost as much as 70 to 80 percent of its population. To make matters worse, several diseases were often introduced into an area at the same time, making the death rate even higher.

People in farming villages were hit the hardest because there were more people living in a smaller amount of space and the disease could be transmitted faster. War, famine, and forced labor all helped make Indians weaker and more vulnerable to disease. Farming villages in Kansas, Nebraska, Texas, and the Dakotas suffered the greatest losses.

The total numbers of Indians who died from epidemic diseases are staggering. In 1638 alone, forty thousand out of sixty thousand Pueblos died. Two years later another ten thousand died and by 1790, only nine thousand Pueblos remained. This same pattern of death by epidemic disease could be found all over the West.

How the Horse Changed North America

While the introduction of epidemic diseases to North America had devastating consequences, the other significant Spanish import, the horse, opened up tremendous opportunities, particularly for hunting.

By 1700 all the Plains tribes of Texas had horses, and from there, horses gradually spread northward across the Missouri River and then westward to the Pacific Ocean.

The biggest impact the horse had on Indian culture was the transformation of farming, or horticultural, tribes into nomadic tribes that roamed the plains hunting buffalo. Not all tribes who acquired the horse gave up farming, however. Some tribes, like the Pawnee and Wichita, roamed the plains just twice a year on buffalo hunts and maintained their farms and villages the rest of the year.

American Indians had hunted buffalo long before the Spanish introduced the horse to North America, but the horse made buffalo hunting much more efficient. Not only did it make catching the buffalo easier, but it also enabled the hunters to carry the meat and hides, as well as their teepees and food, on long hunts.

Horses also made it easier for the nomads to raid Indian farming villages and increased the conflicts between tribes. As diseases took their hardest toll on the villages, nomadic tribes such as the Comanche started to dominate the

A Great Plains Indian on horseback pursues a buffalo.

plains. Their victims were most often the Pueblo, Plains Apache, and Navajo. The Sioux came to dominate the Missouri Valley and eventually forged an alliance with the Arapaho and Cheyenne. By the time explorers and settlers from the eastern U.S. were starting to head west in the mid-nineteenth century, these three tribes had become the most powerful force on the northern and central plains.

While disease weakened the Indian cultures of North America and the introduction of the horse radically improved the lives of those that survived, another factor had a significant impact on American Indian life: the demand for trade goods such as furs and precious metals by the U.S. and Europe. Explorers, fur trappers, and traders would demand permanent access to Indian forests, rivers, mountains, and valleys, and sometimes they would drive Indians out of their lands entirely. They would also force Indians to accept goods and services in trade for what they wanted — whether the Indians wanted these goods and services or not. These foreigners would continue to view Indian cultures as less civilized than their own — and they would continue to impose their own social, cultural, and religious values on any Indians who crossed their paths.

Horses and a woman's work

In both the nomadic and farming tribes, the arrival of the horse introduced new and demanding chores to what made up women's work. For example, it became the woman's job to feed and groom the horses. Finding food in the fall and winter was difficult and time consuming. It was also the woman's job to treat and tan the buffalo hides. With a horse, a hunter could kill four or five buffalo on a single run. His part was dangerous — but it was also exciting, and it was over quickly. Tanning the hide and drying the meat (the woman's job), however, could take over three full days for each buffalo that was killed.

The horse also increased the popularity of polygamy (the practice of having more than one wife) among Indians. By the mid-nineteenth century, more and more successful hunters found they needed extra wives to tan the extra hides.

An Indian raiding party on settlers' cattle.

CHAPTER TWO

Arrival of the European Imperialists

By the eighteenth century, the most powerful countries in Europe were busy carving up the continents of Africa, Asia, and North and South America to create their rival empires. The purpose of having foreign colonies, they felt, was to supply the mother country with wealth, natural resources like gold and silver, and goods such as tobacco and furs. If these were resources the mother country could also sell to other European countries, their colonies would be worth even more.

Colonies, however, were often large and difficult to govern. Many needed to be defended from constant attack by rival European powers or by local natives. The mother country often discovered that her colonies cost more to defend than their resources were worth. In spite of that, these European empires continued to compete for colonial power wherever they could get a foothold. In North America at the beginning of the eighteenth century, the major areas of rivalry were the Northwest Territory, California, the Southwest, and the Pacific Northwest. The main European competitors for these areas were Spain, England, France, and Russia.

Spain's Unsteady Foothold in the West

Spain was the first European power to gain a stronghold in the North American West, but by the mid-eighteenth century, Spain seemed to have enemies on every front. The small Indian villages they took over north of the Rio Grande were so isolated that the Spaniards could not depend on receiving supplies from their main stronghold in Mexico City. Although the Spaniards entered the American Southwest as conquerors, they soon had to forge an alliance with the native Pueblo cultures to survive.

The nomadic Apache tribes were an ongoing problem for Spain, raiding their missions and stealing their horses. Comanche and Wichita tribes were also a threat. These and other tribes raided the Spanish for food, livestock, and horses, and the Spanish in turn raided these Indian tribes for slaves. To make matters worse for the Spanish, they also had the French to contend with.

Pere Marquette, Louis Joliet, and Indians explore the Mississippi.

The French Threaten the Spanish

The French colonists concentrated on exploring North America's inland waterways. The first French explorer in the New World was Jacques Cartier, who sailed up the St. Lawrence River in 1534. In 1673, Pere Marquette and Louis Joliet traveled by birch canoe down from the Great Lakes on what they called "the Great Water" (the Mississippi River). The French traders who followed the paths of these explorers were called voyageurs, and as they paddled their canoes up and down America's waterways, their goal was to dominate the fur trade. French exploration reached its height when Sier de La Salle (Robert Cavelier) reached the Gulf of Mexico in 1682. La Salle claimed as New France the expanse of land west of the Appalachian Mountains to the Mississippi River, and south from Canada to the Gulf of Mexico. By 1699, the French had established colonies from Canada to Louisiana.

With the explorations of La Salle, Marquette, and Joliet, the French had a strong hold on the interior of North America by the 1680s. But like other Europeans, they wanted more. They wanted the fur trade and the rich mines of the American West.

In the early 1700s, the French advanced west from Louisiana and Illinois. Their main tactic was to arm certain Indian tribes (the Pawnee, Wichita, Taovaya, Oto, and other tribes) against the Spanish. They also aided these Indians against warring Apache raiders. In return, these tribes helped the French push up the river valleys into the Great Plains.

The rivalry between France and Spain became complicated with their ever-changing alliances with various Indian tribes. For example, the Apache and the Spanish often fought together against the French in some areas while they were fighting each other just a few miles away. The rivalry became even more complicated when the English started competing with the French and Spanish for inland trade routes.

How the Rivalry for Trade Affected Indian Villages

The main interest of European imperialists, whether they were French, Spanish, English, or Russian, was in controlling trade. They soon found that the best sites for trading were the villages where the lives of both the nomadic, hunting Indians and the more settled farming Indians connected.

Goods that were actively traded included silver, metal tools, guns, corn, buffalo robes, beaver furs, cloth, horses, and dried meat. The way these goods changed hands varied, too. There was direct trade, ritual gift exchanges — and a lot of theft. Sadly, these "goods" often included human beings — slaves.

The Spanish tried to control the exchange points to keep the flow of goods going south toward their stronghold in Mexico. The French tried to divert the flow so goods flowed east to their trading posts along the Mississippi River. The few English traders in the area tried to direct their goods north toward the Hudson Bay area and their strongholds. All of these factors added the threat of violence to frontier trade for both Europeans and Indians. But it was the Indians who really suffered from these trade rivalries. They were often driven from their villages, had their crops looted or burned, or were made into slaves to satisfy the European slave trade. Often Indian villages were forced to trade for goods they did not want or need.

A European missionary preaches to the Indians.

Both the Spanish and the French tried to control Indians with missions they set up to convert the natives to Christianity. Spiritual beliefs have traditionally been very important to these Indian cultures, and they often absorbed new beliefs without letting go of their old ones. So for the most part, Indians in North America did not at first resist Christianity. They were curious about the spiritual beliefs of the white men, and they were polite and courteous listeners when missionaries tried to preach to them.

In most traditional Indian cultures, spirituality is rooted in nature. They believe the land they live on is sanctified, and that the earth, the heavens, and the four directions all have supernatural powers. Indians have a reverence for all aspects of nature and believe that their spiritual leaders receive guidance from unseen spirits. These spirits are everywhere: in caves, in springs, in trees, and in animals. (In fact, many Indians believe that there had once been a golden age when humans and animals lived and talked together.) So it was not hard for many Indians to include prayers to the white man's Son of God in their own religious rituals. But for most European missionaries, especially those from Spain, this interest and courtesy were not enough. They wanted the Indians to give up their own traditional religions and to be exclusively devoted to God as white men understood the concept of god.

The French pulled their missionaries out of the American West and stopped being a threat to the Spanish after 1763, when they lost the French and Indian War to England. The peace treaty

Indian-French interactions

The explorers, hunters, trappers, traders, and missionaries from France interacted differently than the Spanish with native American cultures. The French did most of their exploring in North America along river routes, and therefore interacted most with tribes and cultures that could be reached via these waterways. Jesuit missionaries often went along with French traders on explorations of new river routes. The tended to treat the Indians humanely and to respect the way they lived. To the Indians, the French were often considered to be the most friendly of the foreign explorers and traders.

While the Spanish would accept marriages between Indians and whites if they had to, they basically considered American Indians to be pagan and inferior. Most of the French explorers and traders, on the other hand, had respect for Indian life and an interest in Indian language and culture. They often adopted Indian customs and intermarried with local tribes (although a number of French traders exploited Indians by taking Indian women back to France as slaves). The French were for the most part more interested in developing their fur trade than in building up a powerful empire in the New World.

awarded England all of Canada, as well as all land lying between the Appalachians and the Mississippi, along with east and west Florida.

Although the Spanish traders no longer had to worry about competing with the French, they found they had two new rivals to worry about: the British and the Russians.

Competition for Trade Grows in the Pacific Northwest

In addition to the territory they received from the French in the Mississippi Valley, the British were also interested in the rich fur trade along the northern Pacific coast. Russia, which had already claimed Alaska as its colony, was also interested in establishing trading posts along the north Pacific coast.

The magnificent forests of the north Pacific Coast region were responsible for producing more than a wide variety of quality animal furs. These forests helped the native cultures create a unique and highly developed form of architecture not found anywhere else in the American West. Most of the tribes used beams and planks from these forests to erect homes and buildings of worship. They carved huge, ornate totem poles and hollowed-out canoes.

Ocean currents have always brought a warm climate to the northern Pacific coast. The combination of fair weather and excellent rivers made this area rich in freshwater fish as well as furs. The warm coastal waters were also rich in sea otters and in ocean fish, particularly salmon. In fact, salmon fishing was so important for many of these coastal tribes that it became the center of both their economic and spiritual lives. Because these tribes held annual First Salmon ceremonies and festivals to bless the fishing seasons, they came to be called the Salmon Cultures. To European traders in the mid-eighteenth century, the salmon was less important than the sea otter. The profits that could be made in trading otter skins soon made the Pacific Northwest one of the busiest trading spots in the New World.

Why a Captain Named Cook Alarmed the Spanish

In 1778 a British expedition led by Captain James Cook sailed around the tip of South America and up along the Pacific West Coast, docking at Nootka Sound on Vancouver Island in the Pacific Northwest. Captain Cook's intention was to buy otter skins from the local Indians in Vancouver to make into warm clothing for the expedition further north.

A trader and Indian weighing furs.

What he discovered was that he could purchase fifteen hundred otter skins for practically nothing — the same otter skins he knew would sell in China for one hundred dollars apiece. The news spread quickly to other English merchantmen, who wasted no time taking advantage of the opportunity. This really alarmed the Spanish, because they considered the California coast to be *their* territory.

News of Cook's fur bargains even spread to the newly independent thirteen United States, and American traders were right behind the British. By 1792, American traders from New England were seriously competing for the otter skin trade on the Northwest Coast, and by the late 1790s they dominated it. The Indians called these Americans "Bostons" because they had set sail from Boston Harbor.

Unfortunately, the Americans brought more than just trade to the Indians of the Pacific Northwest. They also brought syphilis and smallpox. The destruction these diseases caused in the Northwest was every bit as terrible as it had been when the Spanish brought their diseases into California.

In 1789 a Spanish expedition seized three British ships that were trading in Nootka, an act that just about brought Britain and Spain to war. But in 1790, the Spanish backed down and granted the British some trade rights along the Spanish coast. As British and American trade increased in the Pacific Northwest, the Spanish slowly retreated.

Captain James Cook.

The Russians Land in California

Spain was also worried about the Russians, who had already established colonies in Alaska. Russian explorers sent in search of furs and trade routes skipped the Pacific Northwest region altogether and concentrated instead on the coast of northern California. They established a post at Fort Ross north of San Francisco Bay in 1812 and used it to supply their colonies in Alaska. The Russians remained in Fort Ross until 1841, the year they sold their livestock and buildings to a Swiss adventurer named John Sutter — the same John Sutter who later played an important part in the California Gold Rush of 1848.

Although the Russians were never much of an actual threat, the Spanish took care to fortify their outposts in California against a possible Russian

The slavers of Nootka

Because the north Pacific coast was so rich in salmon and fur-bearing animals, the Indian tribes in this region were wealthy and experienced traders long before the Europeans showed up. In some ways, their cultures were advanced. These Indians valued art and created masks, toys, helmets, figurines, and jewelry out of wood, ivory, bone, and a soft stone called argillite. They created elaborate and colorful clothing woven from goat hair and cedar bark and decorated their buildings and canoes with ornate wood carvings.

But in some ways, these same tribes were so barbaric that they appalled even the European slave traders. Like the Europeans, they divided themselves into social classes of commoners, nobles, and royalty, with wealth deciding who belonged to which class. Neighboring tribes were always at war, stealing food and furs from each other and taking slaves. The most royal, therefore, were not only the wealthiest — they were the ones with the most slaves.

What appalled the Europeans wasn't that they took slaves. It was how they treated their slaves. It was not uncommon, for example, for a chief to have a slave killed and buried (for luck) with the sinking of a new house post, or to welcome visitors by having their canoes dragged over a beach covered with the bodies of slaves who had been slaughtered just for that purpose. The horrified Europeans claimed they killed *their* slaves only if they had a good reason.

takeover. The real threat to Spanish control in California and the Pacific Northwest (as well as in Texas and the Southwest) was not the British, the Americans, or the Russians. It came from inside the Spanish empire.

The Decline of Spanish Control in North America

After an eleven-year struggle for independence from Spanish rule, Mexican revolutionaries in Mexico City forced the Spanish Viceroy to surrender and won their independence in 1821. The new government guaranteed equality for all Mexican citizens and declared that Catholicism would be Mexico's only recognized religion.

The new country of Mexico covered a lot more territory than the Mexico we know today. The country south of the Rio Grande was divided into equal Mexican states (somewhat like the states that make up the United States of America), but the former Spanish territories to the north (what is today California, Utah, Arizona, New Mexico, Texas, and parts of Colorado) were not. Instead of granting these territories statehood, the new central government of Mexico tried to impose *more* control and make them even more economically dependent.

People started revolting in California, Texas, and New Mexico, people who were angry about high taxes, the poor economy, and the unfair class divisions that kept the rich wealthy and the poor in poverty. They were also angry about the protection the government gave the Catholic Church, which many people thought already had too much power over their lives, and too much of the country's wealth. The economic and social conditions became so bad in its northern territories that the Mexican government decided to reverse the previous Spanish policy and open its borders to foreign trade, hoping that this would improve the economy. This trade, especially with Mexico's neighbor, the U.S., would have a major impact on both Mexico and the development of the American West.

Mexican Trade with the U.S.

The busiest trading spot in northern Mexico proper was Santa Fe on the Rio Grande River. When the Mexican government lifted its trade restrictions, American traders quickly arrived in Santa Fe with entire pack trains loaded with goods they knew Mexicans wanted — clothing, cotton cloth, lace, jewelry, furniture, china, musical instruments, tobacco, and spices. The traders were also anxious to purchase goods, like Mexican gold, silver, horses, woolens, furs, cowhides, and mules. The Americans easily sold all their goods at profits of 500-600 percent, and the road to Santa Fe became known as "the Turquoise Trail."

The Mexican government imposed taxes and customs fees on these imports, but many of the local government officials demanded additional bribes before they allowed the American merchandise to be sold in Santa Fe. Americans who protested often found themselves in jail with their goods confiscated. In addition to the traders, another group of Americans came down the commerce trails to Santa Fe: the mountain men. Beaver hats were a fashionable status symbol in the eastern U.S. and Europe in the early 1800s, and mountain men were trappers who specifically hunted beaver. The market was a profitable one until the fashion trend changed from beaver to silk by the 1840s.

Artists and reporters tended to romanticize the lives these mountain men lived, making them seem to be exciting and heroic. In reality, a trapper's life was filled with danger and hardships. The Rocky Mountains were deadly cold in the winter, and the loneliness was often hard to endure. Grizzly bears and other wild animals could maul a trapper pretty badly, if not actually kill him. After they had trapped almost all of the beaver in the northern Rockies, the mountain men headed toward the Southwest. Santa Fe rapidly became the center of the beaver fur trade. Some of these trappers went to any lengths to get beaver pelts, including crossing the burning desert, fighting Indians, and even becoming Mexican citizens to avoid paying import fees in Santa Fe.

While traders were venturing westward with Mexico's consent, other forces were at work that would push U.S. borders westward: expansion was becoming a political issue in Congress.

The U.S. Expands Its Territory and Federal Power

By 1800 the border of the newly independent United States was only as far west as the Appalachian Mountains. Britain occupied Canada to the north; Spain was in Mexico on the south, and France owned the Louisiana Territory to the west. From 1800 to 1853, the United States actively sought to expand its western border, partly to strengthen its defense against these surrounding European powers, and partly to increase its trade resources.

The Louisiana Purchase. The Louisiana Purchase of 1803 was not only a good real estate deal for the United States, it was good politics. Napoleon, ruler of France, was plotting ways to make France a more powerful colonial power, and with France, Spain, and Britain at each other's throats, President Jefferson was concerned that the U.S. would be caught in the middle. It didn't take long for that fear to be realized.

When Napoleon ordered his governing officials in New Orleans to close the mouth of the Mississippi River to any further American trade, Jefferson immediately proclaimed that in trying to control the Mississippi's access to the ocean, France was declaring itself to be America's enemy. He immediately started negotiating to buy the territory to remove this possible threat. It didn't take long to arrange a deal because Napoleon, as it turned out, was desperate.

It seems Napoleon's army had just been wiped out on Santo Domingo in the Caribbean by fever and Black guerrilla fighters, and he was convinced that he would soon be fighting a war with England in which he would probably lose all of Louisiana anyway. He offered the Louisiana territory for the low sum of $15 million and the agreement of the U.S. government to take over any claims an American might have against France.

Exactly what the U.S. was buying for this $15 million was not very clear. All of the eastern boundaries of the territory were in dispute, and along the western boundaries it was even more confusing. No one was sure where Texas and New Mexico stopped and Louisiana began. It was also not entirely clear what Jefferson planned to do with the territory, or even if he had the

Jim Bridger, mountain man and teller of tall tales, who may have been the first white person to see the Great Salt Lake.

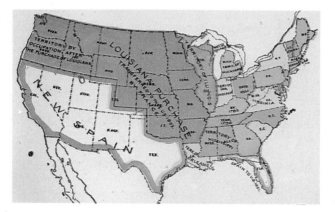

The purple on this map delineates the territory obtained by the Louisiana Purchase, while the orange identifies the territory held by Spain.

constitutional authority to make the purchase in the first place.

The purchase of the Louisiana Territory effectively removed France from North America for good. The purchase also caused the U.S. government to make its position regarding the expansion of its borders clear for itself and for the rest of the world.

U.S. Philosophy of Manifest Destiny. President Jefferson envisioned the United States as an "empire of liberty" when he purchased the Louisiana Territory. He believed that the nation should expand its borders westward as far as the Pacific Ocean. But in spite of Jefferson's personal belief and the fact that many people began migrating westward as early as the first part of the 1800s, *expansionism* (the belief the nation should actively try to expand its borders) was not yet the official policy of the U.S. government.

In the 1840s, a new group of pro-expansion politicians tried to get more Americans enthusiastic about expanding U.S. borders further west. They wanted the U.S. to include not only Texas and Oregon, but Canada, Mexico, Cuba, and other Caribbean countries that were part of the North American continent. To get more support, an extreme expansionist (who was also a New York newspaperman) named John O'Sullivan wrote a long-winded argument that basically said that all these lands belonged to the United States already by reason of "manifest destiny." According to O'Sullivan, God himself had ordained that it was the future destiny of the U.S. to develop "a great experiment of liberty and federal self-government."

The concept of manifest destiny was for the most part just a national propaganda slogan. The politicians who pushed for territorial expansion did so out of fear of the country's surrounding enemies. No one really believed that being entitled to dominate the North American continent was the destiny of *all* U.S. citizens. That destiny was reserved only for those who were white, male landowners. Many people believed that Indians should be removed from the land and that African- and Asian-Americans were not first-class citizens. This concept certainly did not include women, who in most states did not even win the right to vote until 1920. Manifest destiny was, however, the reason the U.S. government gave to justify many subsequent acts of war and aggression, both inside and outside its national boundaries.

By the mid-nineteenth century, most white Americans believed that it was God's will for them to take over and rule the entire continent. Indians generally thought of themselves as custodians — certainly not rulers — of the land they lived on.

To the Indians, the concept of "manifest destiny" meant there was no hope of saving their lands and very little hope of saving their tribal cultures. The expansionists nominated a southern Democrat for President in 1844 named James K. Polk. Polk's entire election campaign was based on his belief that the U.S. Congress should vote to make the territories of both Texas and Oregon official territories of the United States. The expansionists also wanted California.

U.S. Fights Mexico for Texas Territory

After Mexico gained its independence from Spain, it established a new policy of promoting American immigration into Texas by offering immigrants free land in exchange for citizenship. By 1823, there were already three thousand illegal U.S. aliens in the Mexican territory of Texas, and Mexico wanted these people loyal to Mexico, not the U.S.

By 1830, the number of American immigrants in Texas numbered over seven thousand. By this time, there were twice as many Americans living in Texas as there were Mexicans. Instead of becoming more loyal to Mexico, these American immigrants became increasingly anxious to be independent of Mexican rule. Many Texans believed that the U.S. should annex the territory of Texas and make it a U.S. state, and they sent people to Washington to propose the idea to the president.

In 1834, when General Antonio López de Santa Anna became dictator of Mexico, revolts broke out in all of the provinces, including Texas. Santa Anna personally led forces into Texas to put down the revolt, winning an easy victory at the battle of the Alamo and ordering the execution of 371 rebel prisoners in a town called Golidad. Santa Anna did not, however, entirely squash the resistance, and the revolts continued over the next ten years.

In 1844, a Texan named Sam Houston defeated Santa Anna's troops in a battle at the San Jacinto River. Santa Anna was forced to sign an agreement giving full independence to the former Mexican territory of Texas. This was the same year the pro-expansion candidate Polk was elected president of the United States. Polk was eager to offer Texas U.S. statehood, and in February of 1846 Texas accepted the offer and joined the Union.

Mexico had refused to recognize Texan independence in 1844, so it's not surprising that Mexico was upset when Texas became a U.S. state in 1846. President Polk made matters even worse when he insisted that the new Texas-Mexico border be the Rio Grande River instead of the Nueces River, which

The defense of the Alamo during the war with Mexico.

was further north. Polk sent U.S. troops to protect this border, hoping that Mexico had too many of its own internal problems to want to fight about it. Polk was wrong. When Mexico refused to accept the new border and sent troops of its own in May of 1846, Polk convinced Congress to declare war on Mexico.

By the fall of 1846, U.S. troops were winning nearly all of the battles in their drive deeper and deeper into Mexican territory. They had conquered Mexico City but were unable to come to any terms of settlement because the

A Pony Express rider. The Pony Express carried the mail across the country in an average time of ten days, using horsemen riding in relays of thirty-five to seventy miles each.

Mexican government itself was in a state of collapse. The U.S. was divided in its feelings about the war at this point. The expansionists wanted the government to stop trying to negotiate and simply take over all of Mexico. But when it became obvious that Polk was inventing stories of Mexican attacks on U.S. troops just to stir up enthusiasm for the war, many Americans started to object to Polk's war policy. They argued that the United States was being as imperialistic as the Europeans had been, that the U.S. was *not* fighting a war in defense of liberty — it was fighting a war of *conquest* (a war that, in fact, the U.S. had actually started).

Many northerners objected to the Mexican War on the grounds that it would open much more territory to slavery. Northerners also felt that they were paying far more than their share of the costs of the war. Other Americans objected to the war for racial reasons: they didn't want the addition of so many nonwhites to the U.S. population.

In the spring of 1847 anti-war opposition at home caused Polk to accept a treaty that only awarded the U.S. the territories of Texas (north of the Rio Grande), California, and New Mexico (which included what is now Utah and Arizona). Polk was furious, but he knew he had no choice.

U.S. Annexes the Oregon Territory

Texas was only one of President Polk's expansionist conquests. While war was brewing with Mexico over the territory of Texas, Polk was also setting his sights on the substantial territory in the Pacific Northwest that belonged to England.

At first the expansionists wanted to annex Oregon up to the 54° 40' north latitude and were willing to fight England for it. (One of the campaign slogans in the national elections of 1844 was "Fifty-four Forty or Fight.") But the English would not accept a border so far north, and the United States eventually compromised on the forty-ninth parallel. By that time, the U.S. was already at war with Mexico and compromised because it didn't want to risk a war with England as well.

On June 10, 1846, Congress ratified a treaty annexing that portion of the Oregon Territory to the United States. There was just one more major territorial acquisition the U.S. needed to make, and that came in 1853.

U.S. Negotiates the Gadsden Purchase

The U.S. decided it needed a strip of land about 29,000 miles square along what is now the southern Arizona border for a much-needed southern railroad route and sent James Gadsden to Mexico to negotiate the purchase. Mexico had no objections because it felt the land in question was nothing but barren desert anyway. After the purchase, the boundaries of what is now the American West were completely established.

Exploration of the West

Indian tribes living on the North American continent must have been amused at the idea that European immigrants believed they had "discovered" the very land the Indians had been living on for thousands of years. Expeditions sent to explore the West made discoveries only in the sense that this territory was new and unknown to the people who had immigrated to this continent. It was certainly not undiscovered or unexplored to the Indians who already lived here.

While explorers may not have found undiscovered places, they did gather and record a tremendous amount of scientific and geographic knowledge that was in turn made available to many other people. The scientists who were involved in these expeditions believed that their efforts and their journals were furthering the progress of humankind.

Even after the territories were made a part of the United States, expeditions continued to be sent to explore the West. Some were funded by the government, some by the Army, and some by private companies. There were even smaller, independent expeditions that set out to explore on their own. Some of the expeditions kept detailed records of their journeys; others only carried their experiences in their heads. These were no longer the expeditions of Europeans seeking colonial trade routes. These were now expeditions of the American West by Americans.

Despite the largely scientific nature of these expeditions, many, particularly the government expeditions, were more spy missions than anything else. In 1806, for example, U.S. General James Wilkinson ordered Lieutenant Zebulon Pike to lead an expedition across the southern plains, supposedly to find the source of the Red River. What Wilkinson actually wanted was for Pike to spy on the city of Santa Fe (at that time still part of Mexico's northern territories) just in case the U.S. needed to send troops there if war broke out with Mexico.

Other military expeditions were organized in the 1840s when the U.S. Army created the Corps of Topographical Engineers. This was a separate segment of the Army that answered directly to Congress and to the President. The officers of this corps had both scientific and military training and were sent to draw up detailed geographical maps and surveys. Later, in the 1860s and 1870s, this same Corps of Topographical Engineers would be called on to develop maps and surveys specifically to help the Army locate and defeat American Indians.

Each of these expeditions in its own way contributed to the knowledge the settlers would need as they began their westward migrations. While they may have provided records and maps to make the journey easier for settlers, they failed to show that these were not empty vistas of wild western frontier just waiting to be tamed by heroic and adventurous European-Americans; these were the homelands of many Indian cultures that depended on the forests and wildlife to survive. These maps and records also did little to explain the hardships and danger the settlers could expect to encounter on their journeys.

In this nineteenth-century photo, a covered wagon train stretches toward the horizon.

CHAPTER THREE

Settlement and Growth

The city of Santa Fe was a flourishing trade center long before the Southwest became part of the United States, and it was one of the first destinations of Americans who traveled west to make their fortunes.

Enterprising merchants who made the eight-hundred-mile trip southwest from Missouri to Santa Fe usually traveled by covered wagon. For the most part, only men attempted this dangerous overland trip, staying in Santa Fe only long enough to trade their cloth, furniture, tobacco, and other goods for Mexican beaver, silver, and gold. These American traders traveled in long caravans of fifty to one hundred wagons each to protect themselves against raiding parties of Cheyenne, Kiowa, and Comanche Indians. The journey was not only dangerous, it was slow. If these traders were lucky, their wagons could cover fifteen miles a day, which meant the journey usually took them at least two months.

The young U.S. was greedy and had an appetite for trade. Adventurous trappers forged more and more trails, opening up trading passages leading further and further west. The Gila River and Old Spanish Trails led all the way from Missouri to San Diego and Los Angeles on the Pacific Ocean. Trappers and traders were only the first of many to travel these trails. The great rush of American settlers streaming west for land and gold would follow them thirty to forty years later.

Many trappers knew that the market for beaver skins would not last forever. They were smart enough to realize that Americans who heard about the rich farmland in the Northwest would want to move there. So they started building forts along such passages as the Oregon Trail (which led from Independence, Missouri, to Fort Vancouver in the Oregon Territory) to sell supplies to the wagon trains of people who would soon be heading west. Some trappers promoted frontier fever. Their stories about the lush Oregon valleys had people back east excited about the idea of farming out west.

The Overland Migrations

Searching for the American Dream. The explosion of immigrants came soon thereafter. Missionaries, merchants, and settlers who were hungry for farmland flooded into territory that had previously been populated only by American Indians and descendants of the Spanish conquistadors. For over a half century, millions of Anglo-Americans, African-Americans, European immigrants, Mexican immigrants, and even a substantial number of Chinese transformed both the social and physical landscape of the American West.

These migrations brought animals, seeds, and money. But even more important, they brought women. The presence of wives, sisters, and daughters meant that instead of making a quick fortune and returning east, many of the men would be putting down roots and raising a family. (An exception to this was the Gold Rush of 1849, a migration made up almost entirely of single men who were heading for California to strike it rich.)

For most immigrants heading west, the "jumping off" point was Independence, Missouri. Here they would gather with other immigrants on acres of land outside the city, where they would assemble their wagons with the possessions and provisions they would take on their journey.

Life on the Trail. Whatever the settlers needed to start their new lives they had to carry with them. This often included a bull and several cows, hogs, chickens, a plow and harness, and all their household goods. Most of the migrants overestimated the capacity of their animals to pull that kind of a load and the trails became littered with the items they had to abandon along the way. Grindstones, baking ovens, kegs, barrels, clothing, iron safes, even bacon and beans, appeared along the trails.

Settlers make camp along the trail.

The trip itself was much harder on women than on the men. When families traveled together, they divided the work up pretty much the same way it was divided back home. But since the ordinary, daily farm work was now impossible, the men only had to drive the wagons, take care of the livestock, select the route, and make any necessary repairs. Getting up at 4:00 a.m. to harness the livestock and walking along a loaded wagon for eighteen hours was hard work, but the women had it even worse. Once they stopped for the evening, the men could rest. But the women had to haul water and collect firewood to cook dinner. Then they had to prepare the lunch they would eat on the trail the next day. After cleaning up, the women washed clothes, did the mending, and took care of the children. The next morning, it was their job to get up before the men to cook breakfast.

It is estimated that about ten thousand people died making these migrations, which is about 3 percent of the total that set out. (The death rate of the U.S. society as a whole at that time was 2.5 percent.) Contrary to the way these migrations are portrayed in western movies, attacks by Indians were not the primary cause of death. In fact, attacks by Indians were rare and usually only on wagons traveling alone or in pairs. (Records show that between 1840 and 1860, only 362 whites were killed by Indians on the trail. Those same records show that whites killed 426 Indians.)

Accidents accounted for more deaths than did Indian attacks, but by far the main cause of death was disease brought on in part by poor sanitation and medical care. Although diphtheria killed many people on the trail (mostly children), cholera was the major killer. The cholera epidemic of 1850-1852 killed half of all the people who would die on the trails between 1840 and 1860. One wagon train reported that its members dug one grave every eighty yards. A pioneer described it as being "250 miles from the nearest post office, 100 miles to wood, 20 miles to water, and six inches from hell."

Remarkably, the harsh physical conditions did not weaken the spirit or the determination of most settlers. Although some incidents of crime and violence occasionally broke out among the members of these wagon trains, most of the time they acted as a close-knit community, exchanging information and helping each other as best they could.

Wagons were not the only popular form of transportation. Many people traveled by steamboat. These boats could negotiate in water as shallow as four feet and carried freight and passengers up and down the Ohio, Mississippi, and Missouri Rivers. The steamboat was fast and powerful, and it had a flat bottom that allowed it to carry heavy loads of passengers and freight even in shallow parts of the river. But it was also dangerous, and many travelers considered steamboats a bad risk, believing there was a one in three chance they would sink, explode, or go up in flames with everyone on board (which they often did). Some people preferred to travel to California on huge clipper ships, by way of the Panama Canal or around Cape Horn at the southern tip of South America. Other people made the trip overland on mule carts.

Patterns of Migration. Some people chose to migrate west for adventure and quick fortune. Others wanted the free land and a chance to make a better life for their families. There were as many different reasons for migrating as there were immigrants. But there were some patterns to the flow, too.

For example, migrants who were born in the U.S. tended to settle in the same general latitude out west as the place they left. Settlers from South Carolina would migrate to Texas, but not usually to North Dakota. This makes sense from a farmer's point of view, because the animals and seeds they brought with them were adapted to the climate they left behind and would not do well in a place that was substantially warmer or colder, wetter or drier.

The U.S. citizens that chose to migrate were for the most part fairly prosperous. Even though the land was often free to settlers, poorer farmers and businessmen could not afford the cost of moving themselves and their belongings across country, building a new house and farm when they got to their destination, and then supporting their families until their first crops came in. If a poor man did choose to come west, he usually had to work as a laborer for a railroad or mining company for two or three years until he could afford to send for his family. It was even worse for poor single women, unless they planned to work as a schoolteacher or prostitute, although a number of single women did overcome the difficulties of migrating west on their own and established successful farms.

Although most of the people who migrated west in the nineteenth century were farmers, the migrations affected more than just agriculture. There were spectacular mineral rushes (primarily for gold and silver) that created mining camps and towns like Denver, Colorado, that eventually became prosperous cities. In the Rocky Mountains and on the Pacific Coast, the first settlers often built their first houses grouped together in towns before they started to farm the surrounding land. Cities in the West became as important as rural farming communities.

American migrants also proved to be a restless people, usually moving two or three times before finally settling in one spot. This was true regardless of the person's ethnic background and whether or not they were farmers. About the only reason settlers had for staying in one place was wealth. The successful people in a new settlement usually stayed, while the less successful people moved on.

The majority of people who migrated west were white, native-born Americans, but there were also some very important minority groups as well: foreign-born Europeans, African-Americans (some as slaves, some as freed slaves or freemen), Chinese, Mexicans, and even Canadians.

Regardless of the ethnic backgrounds of the immigrants, the migrations usually fell into one of three categories:

Chinese immigrants panning for gold.

Community migrations (such as those to Oregon) consisted mostly of people who were satisfied with their ways of life but who were dissatisfied with their present opportunities. They believed opportunities out west would be better. Community migrations were usually groups of people who were either related to each other or who had strong community ties with each other back east. These were usually organized by word of mouth and were the most common type of migration.

Utopian migrations (such as the Mormon trek to Utah) were not just interested in maintaining their way of life in a better place. They were interested in creating a utopia — a new and better society, totally separate from the society they had left behind. To achieve this new and "perfect" society, the migrants were willing to change many of the institutions that were basic to American life, such as marriage and democracy.

Migrations to acquire possessions (like the California Gold Rush) were not concerned with finding a new place to recreate an existing way of life or with finding a place to establish a new and better one. They saw the move as a temporary one, going west for the sole purpose of acquiring a fortune and then returning home again to spend it.

Between 1840 and 1860, about 300,000 people traveled west on overland trails. Of them, 53,000 went to Oregon, 200,000 went to California (120,000 during the Gold Rush), and 43,000 went to Utah as Mormons. After 1860, European-Americans tended to migrate west mostly to acquire possessions, while African-Americans and European immigrants continued to migrate as communities to improve their opportunities for making a living. Let's take a closer look at each of these types of westward migrations.

Overland to Oregon — Community Migration

Trappers and explorers returned east from Oregon with stories about rich farmlands and golden opportunities for a better life. In the 1840s and 1850s, these stories circulated in the local newspapers and were repeated by local lecturers all over the East. Many people received enthusiastic letters from friends and relatives who had already made the trip. Because this information was spread by word of mouth, the new groups that formed with the intention of migrating tended to be either relatives or close neighbors of one another.

European migrations to Oregon were organized pretty much the same way. The American West received a lot of attention from European writers and journalists, some of whom portrayed it as a land of savage and hostile Indians, while others wrote enthusiastically about the promise of adventure and opportunity.

Although many Europeans were enjoying an increase in their standard of living in the nineteenth century, more and more of them became dissatisfied with not being able to own land. There simply was not enough land available. The stories they heard about the vast farmlands available on America's western frontier lured the first few European immigrants, who were prosperous enough to pay for both the ocean voyage and the expensive wagon journey overland from America's East Coast. But it wasn't until these first immigrants wrote home and convinced their relatives and friends to follow that substantial numbers of European immigrants made the trip.

In some European countries, terrible economic conditions were the main reason people left for America. For example, in the mid-1840s, a terrible blight attacked Ireland's important potato crop. Over 2 million people died as a result, from disease and starvation. That represented over one-quarter of Ireland's population.

America Fever

Though Europeans were bombarded with all forms of information enticing them to emigrate to the American West, by far the biggest influences were letters from friends and relatives who had already moved. Two million letters reached Britain in 1854 alone. Even tiny Denmark received half a million letters in just a year.

Each letter boasted about the writer's incredible wealth and urged loved ones back home to follow. The impact of these letters was phenomenal; every time one was delivered to a European village, it was a major event.

Once the idea was planted, Europeans became haunted with the idea of making the journey themselves. Many called it the *America Fever*, a virus that left them permanently unhappy with life in the Old World.

Tens of thousands of Irish immigrants migrated to America in search of farmland and the opportunity of making a better life. Unfortunately, by the time they paid for the trip to America, most of them were too poor to move west and buy the necessary land, livestock, and equipment. Instead, they were forced to live in the slums of the larger eastern cities such as Boston and New York. The Irish were hated by Americans who had lived in this country longer than they had, and they were looked down on as a social menace. The few that did manage to go west did so by getting backbreaking laboring jobs on canal and railroad projects, but many people resented the Irish taking even these menial positions. Often companies that were hiring for these projects put up "No Irish Need Apply" signs. (This became so common that it was often abbreviated to just NINA.)

In some European countries, such as Germany, politics played a big part in motivating people to migrate. Between 1830 and 1860, over 1.5 million Germans moved to the United States, many of them unhappy that Europe's 1848 democratic revolutions had failed. America's democracy offered them hope. These German immigrants were often called '48ers and for the most part only migrated as far west as Wisconsin and other parts of the Midwest, where they would eventually become involved in many of this country's progressive political movements.

German immigrants were politically active in their opposition to slavery and political corruption. Even though they were by no means wealthy, they were for the most part better educated than many of the other European immigrants and were great supporters of education, art, and music even on the frontier. But this didn't always make the Germans the best traveling companions or the most welcome neighbors. Many considered themselves to be culturally superior not only to the Irish and other immigrant groups, but to the more established Anglo-Americans as well. Because of this, other ethnic groups considered them snobbish and clannish.

Foreign-born ethnic groups tended to stick together and develop their own networks of migration. For example, communities of Norwegian immigrants in Wisconsin and Minnesota in the early 1800s served as the jumping-off points for other Norwegians who later migrated even further west to North and South Dakota. For the most part, these migrations were closed to anyone who was not Norwegian. The Germans, German-Russians, and Swedes all developed these types of migration networks.

Another group that developed community migration networks was America's native-born African-American community, the Exodusters. Although these migrations were organized through community churches and public meetings (and therefore were community-based migrations), they also often had utopian goals. After the Civil War, thousands of freed Blacks from Kentucky, Tennessee, Louisiana, Mississippi, and Texas came to believe that they could forge a better life by creating a utopian society of Blacks in Kansas — one that was segregated from neighboring white communities but coexisted with them. A seventy-year-old ex-slave named Benjamin "Pap" Singleton was the most important influence on this movement, founding two of the

Clara Brown leads Blacks to Colorado

Once African-American migrants settled in successfully, they often sponsored other Black migrations. Clara Brown was a good example. She purchased her own freedom from slavery in 1859 and then persuaded a group of gold prospectors who were heading west to hire her as a cook. Once she got to Colorado, she started a series of laundries for other prospectors. She was so successful that she could afford to bring thirty-four of her relatives to Denver to join her.

several Black colonies that were established in Kansas. In spite of the violent protests of Southern whites (who were afraid of losing their source of cheap labor), by 1880 over fifteen thousand African-Americans had migrated to Kansas. Smaller communities of African-Americans also appeared in Nevada, Utah, the Pacific Northwest, and elsewhere. Many of the Blacks who settled the West were soldiers in the U.S. Army who came to be stationed out west and then chose to stay there after their military duties were over.

There were two reasons that migrants (whatever their nationality and ethnic background) did not stop and settle in the fertile and accessible farmlands of the Mississippi Valley when there was still plenty of available land. The first was health, and the second was climate.

Outbreaks of diseases such as smallpox, influenza, and cholera were common throughout the U.S. in the middle of the nineteenth century, but they hit the Midwest especially hard. Even worse was malaria, which Americans at that time called the fever or the ague, and a disease called "milk sickness" or "puking fever." It was later discovered that the ague (which gave its victims severe chills and a burning fever at the same time) was spread by mosquitos. Milk sickness, it was later discovered, was caused by eating the meat of cows that had grazed on a plant called white snakeroot.

At the same time, stories were spreading throughout the U.S. that the West — especially the Far West in the Oregon valleys and along the Pacific coast — was a far healthier place to live. The famous writer Samuel Clemens (Mark Twain) wrote that California was so healthy you actually had to leave the state to die. Doctors published articles in medical journals stating that even the journey west in itself could restore a person to good health.

Go west, young man — and stay healthy

In the 1840s, thousands of the immigrants heading toward the Great Plains of the West were convinced the prairie air would restore them to health. Newspapers were full of stories of lifelong invalids who had made miraculous recoveries after only a week or two on the trail. They claimed the West cured everything from liver complaints and gastric ulcers to smallpox, lockjaw, and chronic depression. There were even reports of bedridden people who could suddenly walk. Although most of these reports were grossly exaggerated, the exercise and fresh air migrants experienced on the trail were certainly healthier than the hazardous and unhealthy working conditions and industrial pollution back east.

In reality, some aspects of traveling west were much less healthy. Meals were monotonous and not very nutritious. Most Americans west of the Alleghenies existed on corn and hog meat. The corn was usually in the form of mush, grits, or bread, and the pork was almost always salted. Everything that could possibly be fried was — in lard. In spite of the terrible food, migrants ate impressive quantities. Even worse was what they drank. Coffee and tea were often scarce and milk and water contaminated, and popular alternatives became corn whiskey and apple cider. These dietary habits led to widespread obesity and drunkenness. It also led to some other more bizarre diagnoses. Many physicians at the time seriously believed that the combination of grease and alcohol in some people actually made them flammable and in danger of a condition they called "spontaneous combustion."

Americans also believed the West had a better climate for farming than did either the East or the Midwest. With the mild, wet winters of Oregon and California, farmers no longer had to feed and shelter their animals through a long season of cold weather. This lessened their work, saved them money, and improved their farms' productivity.

Establishment of Protestant Missionaries. Another important motivation for settling the Oregon Territory was to spread "Christianity in the dark and cruel shores of the Pacific," as Hall Jackson Kelley described it. Kelley was a New England schoolteacher who started promoting the colonization of the Pacific Northwest as early as the 1820s, when the English still maintained a strong influence in the area. Kelley wanted Oregon to be American and Protestant, not English, so he did his best to convince Protestant evangelists back east that the Nez Percé, Cayuse, and Flathead Indians of the region needed to be Christianized. While Kelley did succeed in convincing a number of Protestants to establish missionary posts (as well as convince large numbers of Americans to migrate to Oregon), the attempts to convert American Indians to Christianity proved to be a disaster. At first the Indians were polite but uninterested, even when the missionaries moved onto their land. But when the diseases the migrants brought with them spread to the native communities, the Indians no longer ignored them.

The Cayuse blamed a measles epidemic that killed a large number of their children on the missionaries themselves. Because they were afraid these American missionaries would take more of their land and cause more of their people to die from disease, the Indians became hostile and started attacking the missions. In spite of these attacks, however, the missions did succeed in establishing permanent agricultural settlements, especially along the Columbia River. The letters these first settlers sent back to friends and relatives in the East were a major factor in stirring the enthusiasm of the large number of migrants that followed.

The Need for Government Protection. By 1842, America was experiencing Oregon fever. As more and more people signed up for the dangerous wagon train journeys, explorers sought new and safer routes. But whichever routes the migrants chose, they faced the hazards of snowbound mountain passes, treacherous deserts, and American Indians who resisted the encroachment of migrants on their way of life. It was not until 1847, however, that Congress finally had the War Department establish military posts along the route to ensure the safety of the migrants. It took a particularly gruesome experience to convince them.

In April of 1846, an elderly farmer named George Donner left Illinois with eighty-seven migrants bound for Oregon. This small group had only twenty wagons and was badly equipped. Worse yet, neither Donner nor his party had any experience in overland travel. They did manage somehow to survive crossing the Nevada desert, although fighting broke out that led to a murder. That's when their luck ran out. In the fall, when they reached the Sierra Nevada mountains, they were hit with a series of early snowfalls. A few members of the party set out for help while the rest tried to seek shelter. Help did not arrive until January, and by then the food had long since run out. After the cattle died, some members resorted to cannibalism to stay alive. Many others died of exhaustion, starvation, and exposure. Because winter made the pass so hard to reach, it took rescue parties from January through April to bring out the survivors. That part of the Sierra Nevada Mountains is still called the Donner Pass.

The Mormons — a Utopian Migration to Utah

From the time their church was founded in the U.S. in 1830, the Mormons have been one of America's most hated and persecuted religious groups. (Followers of the Church of Jesus Christ of Latter-Day Saints are commonly referred to as Mormons and often refer to themselves as Saints.) They originally settled in Missouri, but in the fall of 1838 a mob of angry Missouri settlers confiscated their property, jailed their leaders, and drove them across the Missouri River to Nauvoo, Illinois.

Their reception in Illinois was not any warmer. In 1844, Mormon homes were ransacked and Joseph Smith, the founder of the Mormon Church, was murdered by a hostile mob. Not surprisingly, church leaders, led by Brigham Young as president of the church's governing Twelve Apostles, became convinced they needed to find a new home for their congregation. Although they considered the more common migrant destinations of Oregon and California, Mormon leaders liked the idea of the arid basin land around the Great Salt Lake near the Rocky Mountains in Utah. They believed that the difficulties they would face building a settlement in such rough country would ensure that they would be free to build their own economic and social order with little outside interference. They knew it would be hard. They had no idea just how hard.

Before they could plant and harvest crops, the Mormons had to build dams and canals to irrigate the bone-dry valleys. Before they could build homes or businesses, they had to build sawmills. Almost all the essentials they needed, such as sugar, cloth, iron, and glass, had to be brought from the East by oxcart, which made these items expensive. But by the fall of 1847, over seventeen hundred Mormons had made it safely to the Great Salt Lake and were enthusiastically building their new lives.

In 1847, the main body of sixteen thousand Mormon immigrants arrived in the Salt Lake valley. Even more important was the impact of the

A Mormon family — a husband with two wives and nine children.

California Gold Rush of 1848. Over thirty thousand gold seekers passed through their valley on the way to California, all of whom spent their money in Salt Lake on food, mining provisions, and blacksmithing services. It was a tremendous boost to the Mormon economy. The Mormons were now actively seeking converts all over the world and helped over thirty thousand new converts migrate from Europe, Australia, the South Pacific, China, Japan, India, and South Africa.

But the Mormons had to face other obstacles besides their new home's harsh mountain and desert terrain. Their leader, Brigham Young, urged the Mormon settlers to interact peacefully with local Indians. Young stated that his policy was to give the Indians presents and to show kindness instead of making war. This policy did not extend to their other neighbors, however. Because of the persecution the Mormons faced in Missouri and Illinois, they called their new home Deseret and designed it to survive in a world of enemies. They wanted the U.S. government to recognize Deseret as a state, but they also wanted to be self-sufficient, and they wanted the right to make their own laws. As a result, many of the church's practices came into direct conflict with the Constitution and laws of the United States and with the powers of the federal government.

In 1852, the Mormons put the issue of states' rights to the test when they announced their doctrine of plural marriages, stating that their church considered it lawful for a man to take more than one wife. They assumed that their right to do this would be protected by the First Amendment of the Constitution, but both Congress and the U.S. Supreme Court voted otherwise and drafted specific laws that made polygamy (or plural marriages) illegal.

Law and order within the Mormon state was beginning to fall apart at this time. A band of Mormon terrorists that called themselves the Danites (or Avenging Angels) rode throughout the Mormon territory promoting murder and revenge against U.S. government officials. Whatever support the Mormons had in Congress quickly disappeared, and in 1857 President Buchanan sent twenty-five hundred men (about one-sixth of the entire U.S. Army) to suppress the rebellion in Utah.

Before the Army could reach Utah, a wagon train of Missouri migrants became angry when the Mormons in southern Utah refused to sell them any supplies. In retaliation, the Missourians committed minor acts of vandalism on Mormon crops and abused some of

Mountain Meadows Massacre.

the local Indians. When the Indians started to attack the Missouri wagon train, the Mormons saw a chance to get revenge. Just as the Indians started to attack, one of the Mormon leaders appeared and advised the migrants that he had persuaded the Indians to let them leave if they surrendered their arms.

When the migrants did surrender, the Mormons and the Indians slaughtered all the adults. They killed 120 altogether, and the Mormons adopted the 17 small children they spared. According to some reports, the Mormons afterward tried unsuccessfully to cover up the incident and to blame it on the Indians. Many people believed this incident was just the start of an oncoming wave of violence and bloodshed.

Aside from this Mountain Meadows Massacre, however, the Mormon War (as it was called) did not have much bloodshed. The Army was unable to reach Utah before bad weather set in and had to spend the winter in the Rockies. By spring, the Mormons withdrew some of their demands and started negotiating for peace. For the next several years federal troops remained in Utah. This turned out to be a benefit to the Mormons, however, who carried on a profitable trade with the seven thousand military personnel and civilians stationed at Camp Floyd.

The Mormons were also able to buy up about $4 million worth of government goods for less than $100,000 in 1860-61 when the garrison had to be reduced due to the outbreak of the Civil War. The State of Deseret remained a "ghost state" governed by federal officials but not quite achieving statehood until 1896, when Utah was formally admitted into the Union.

The California Gold Rush

This type of migration was altogether different than the migration of farmers to Oregon or the migration of Mormons and other groups seeking their own form of utopia. They were organized differently, moved across the country differently, and migrated for different reasons.

It started January 24, 1848, when James Marshall found gold near the lumber mill he had been hired to build on the American River at Coloma. Marshall was inspecting a newly dug channel that diverted the river water to run the mill wheel and spotted some chunks of ore glittering in the soft mud of the channel's banks. When he bit into it to see if it might be gold, it was soft enough for his teeth to leave an impression. When he and his crew saw that more chunks were scattered all over, just waiting to be collected, he excitedly reported the news to the mill's owner, John Sutter.

At first Sutter tried to keep it a secret so it wouldn't interrupt the work on his mill. But within a month all of his laborers had walked off the job and started excavating the stream beds north of Sacramento. It wasn't until May that reports of gold strikes reached San Francisco. By June, San Francisco was virtually a ghost town. People closed their shops and even abandoned ships in the harbor to head out for the diggings. By August, newspapers in the East were carrying the reports of gold strikes. Even though there were claims that the rivers in California were overflowing with gold, many easterners were skeptical about the reports. But in December, the government published an

Gold fever

It was common during the 1840s for newspapers to compare the miners rushing west for gold to sick or insane people. The disease was Gold Fever — and it was incurable. People literally dropped everything they were doing and used their life's savings to pay for the trip west. Friends and relatives who hadn't caught the fever yet called them insane and referred to them as lunatics. A prospector who rode into a western mining town with news of a nearby strike would immediately cause a stampede of the local inhabitants. Indians, who had no use for gold and who had ignored the plentiful nuggets for hundreds of years, were bewildered by all the insanity. The Sioux holy man, Black Elk, called gold the yellow metal that makes the white man crazy.

Panning for gold around 1890.

official report based on the findings of its own agents in California. President James Polk made it even more official when he proclaimed it the find of the century. After that, Americans went crazy with gold fever. Men from every part of the United States rushed to California seeking their share of adventure and easy money.

By fall, news had also spread to Hawaii, Mexico, Peru, and Chili. Not long after that, the fever spread to Europe, Asia, and the rest of the world. By 1849, large numbers of Americans, Europeans, Chinese, Mexicans, and Chileans were streaming into California, increasing the state's non-Indian population from 14,000 to 224,000 by 1852.

The cheapest route from the East was overland. Over thirty thousand walked because they couldn't even afford the price of a wagon. Others preferred to travel by ship through the Panama Canal or around South America's Cape Horn and up the Pacific Coast. The Cape Horn route often took as long as four months.

Unlike the migrations that were organized for Oregon and Utah, the '49ers were not heading west for land, freedom, a gentler climate, or even a better place to raise their families. Almost all of them came with the single of intention of making a fortune and taking it back home with them.

Another way the gold migrations were markedly different was in the number of women and children migrants. Whole families made the journey to Oregon and Utah. But less than 5 percent of all the Gold Rush migrants were women and children.

The California Gold Rush of 1849 (which gave the first prospectors the name '49ers) was only the first of a number of mineral rushes to the West in the 1800s. Tens of thousands flocked to Colorado in 1859, and in 1860 ten thousand California prospectors streamed back east across the Sierra Nevada mountains to the Comstock Lode discovered in Nevada, although it proved to be more profitable for silver than for gold. In 1862, over twenty thousand people rushed to Idaho when news spread of the mineral strikes discovered there. After that, thirty thousand prospectors headed toward Montana in the beginning of 1864. Many of these, of course, were the same prospectors, always rushing toward the next big strike that might bring them their fortunes. Even the Chinese who immigrated in the 1840s fit this pattern of migration.

Although China was suffering through a difficult period of hardship and famine in the mid-1800s, the thousands of Chinese immigrants who bought their steamer tickets for San Francisco fully intended to stay in America only long enough to make their fortunes. They did not come with the expectation of building a better life in a new country, and only one Chinese immigrant in thirteen was a woman.

Chinese workers resting in tent at night.

About two thousand of the prospectors that rushed to California were African-Americans, a number that included slaves as well as freemen. But most of the African-Americans who migrated west in the 1800s followed the community type of migration pattern, moving with friends and family to settle down in a place that offered more economic and social opportunities.

For most of the Gold Rush immigrants of the mid-1800s, their dreams of wealth and fame ended in disillusionment and disappointment. The nuggets of gold that could be found in the stream beds and close to the earth's surface were scooped up pretty quickly. The veins that remained were too deep to mine with just a pick and shovel. The ones who really profited from the California Gold Rush were those who had the money to set up large mining companies with expensive hydraulic machinery   and those who made their money off the prospectors, of course. By 1858, only one-tenth of the original number of gold migrants remained in the West. The rest went home, usually after only a year or two, with little or no gold but a lot of great stories to tell. Those who stayed took other jobs or ended up working for the large mining companies.

The biggest impact of the mineral rushes was how they transformed unpopulated regional outposts into cities like San Francisco and Denver that even rivaled those in the East. These rushes directly led to California's statehood, and they influenced the development of all the Rocky Mountain territories. Even though the madness sparked by the Gold Rush of 1849 gradually faded as the prospectors gave way to big business, the American dream of getting rich quick seemed only to get stronger. Even those who returned home without gold or silver in their pockets spread stories of other riches: the rich earth and open grasslands perfect for farming and raising livestock. Those who stayed helped settle the territories and took advantage of the opportunities the coming of the railroad would bring.

Asian and European workers building the last mile of the Pacific Railroad.

A Multicultural Portrait of the Move West

CHAPTER FOUR

Life in the West

Settlers who migrated with relatives and neighbors formed different types of western settlements than those who migrated to form utopian societies or those who came west just to strike it rich. The Northern European immigrants and American-born settlers who came west for land tended to form orderly, Protestant farming communities that contrasted sharply with the lawless, sprawling mining towns of the prospectors. The European communities were often rich with their unique languages and customs, while Mormon and African-American utopian pioneers built close-knit, spiritual communities around their shared vision of a better life. After these first migrations, work was begun on a transcontinental railroad, and new waves of immigrants, this time from Southern Europe and Asia, poured into the West looking for work.

This tremendous diversity of races and cultures produced significant social, economic, and political problems in the West that are still being felt today. American-born settlers looked down on the European immigrants (especially the Irish and the Jews), and almost everyone considered the Chinese and Indians less than human. Although women started to become vocal about their rights in the nineteenth century, they were still considered inferior to men, and most were not allowed to vote. Children were also considered little more than property and were badly exploited by the industries that sprang up in urban areas toward the end of the century. Let's take a closer look at how these different groups lived and how their differences led to conflict.

Western Communities of European and Asian Immigrants

The first Europeans to migrate to the American West were primarily English-speaking people from England, Scotland, and Wales. As the West opened up, immigrants arrived from all over Europe, although by 1860 the majority were German Protestants and Irish Catholics. The Irish came to the American West to escape the terrible economic conditions in their homeland and to find work. They tended to settle in the larger cities and towns along the railroads they helped build. The Germans built orderly farming communities along the

Chinese laundry worker.

Missouri and Upper Mississippi Rivers and worked to keep their culture alive in their new surroundings. They started up their own newspapers, brewed German beer in the Old World style, and founded German-American friendship groups. They were also quick to enlist when the northern army was recruiting soldiers to fight in the Civil War. Both the Germans and the Irish were known for their political activism and their lively public debates. In the 1860s, Scandinavians started migrating west, and they, like the Germans, came for land, not jobs. The Scandinavians tended to settle in the northern Midwest in communities that reflected their Swedish and Norwegian cultures.

The great rush of Northern European immigrants finally slowed down by the 1880s, just as a new, smaller wave of people was starting. These were primarily Chinese, Italians, and Jews who came to find work mining gold and building the overland railroads.

At first, the Chinese settled in San Francisco, their port of entry, and around the mining communities of northern California, but they eventually found their way into almost every frontier community. Rather than spend

Chinese fongs and huigans

Chinese immigrants who settled in and around San Francisco organized themselves in the U.S. into communities they called *fongs* and *huigans.* Fongs were groups of families that came from the same Chinese village, while huigans were groups of fongs from the same Chinese province or district. Because these huigans operated as a sort of merchant organization in China, they became known as "companies" in the United States, and the six huigans that grouped together in San Francisco came to be known as the Six Companies.

The fongs and huigans did more than provide ethnic ties for the Chinese immigrant community. The Six Companies grew into an organization that provided full time law officials, settled labor disputes, provided defense against Anglo-American harassment, organized housing, and even maintained the religious altars. This community structure was so self-contained that Chinese immigrants were governed and protected with practically no outside interference.

Unfortunately, some of the fongs were set up by powerful Chinese overlords as secret crime organizations involved in prostitution and the opium trade. These, too, operated as extended families in a self-contained community structure similar to the mafia.

time on get-rich-quick schemes, many hard-working Chinese chose instead to start their own businesses, such as laundries and restaurants, and to save up to buy land. Their successes often aroused the resentment of less enterprising settlers in the community. Chinese immigrants also kept their cultural identity more separate than any other immigrant group in the West, forming "Chinatowns" in almost every city. Their strange language and customs, combined with their willingness to work at whatever jobs were available, helped make them the targets of more prejudice and persecution than any other people in the American West, with the exception of the American Indian.

Even the Jews, who had been so persecuted in their European homelands, got along better in the West than the Chinese, although relatively few Jewish immigrants migrated west. Most chose to remain in the larger cities back east. The ones who did migrate west also tended to settle in cities and to take up the same trades and professions they had in Europe, becoming merchants, jewelers, watchmakers, and educators. Although the Jews were not as persecuted in the American West as the Chinese and Indians, they did endure a great deal of anti-Semitism.

Most of the pioneers who headed west in the 1840s were white, native-born Americans. In the late 1860s, after the Civil War ended, African-American migrants also headed west in substantial numbers. Over 60 percent of American-born migrants headed west to farm, with most of the others starting trades like blacksmithing, harnessmaking, and carpentry to provide services to these farmers. A few were doctors, lawyers, and schoolteachers. Most of these migrants were in their early twenties and married when they migrated, settling into their new homesteads with families already underway. Whether these homesteaders were European, Asian, or American born, the settlements they formed were the true frontier communities.

Community Life on the Frontier

Settlers living in a close community looked out for one another and offered each other help in times of need. They traded services, celebrated each others' life changes, and socialized together. Their children identified themselves with the community and tended to marry within it. But a group of people didn't make up a community simply because they lived together in a certain geographical area. To be a community, they had to have things in common that tied them together, such as family ties or jointly owned property or religious convictions. The more ties, the closer the community. The kinship-based migrations we studied in Chapter Three automatically formed close-

That guy's a Lallapalooza!

Nothing reflects the cultural diversity of the West as much as the contributions both settlers and Indians made to the American language.

By 1860, Irish and German immigrants made up the largest bodies of foreign-born immigrants in the United States. An Irish *hoist* was a kick in the pants and *getting one's Irish up* meant getting angry. Americans thought *shenanigans* was a perfect word for mischief, and *lallapalooza* was a great way to describe someone who was exceptionally strong.

The German words that found their way into the language included many words for food and drink, including *pumpernickel, lager, pretzel, frankfurter, hamburger,* and *wienerwurst* (which was later shortened to *wiener*).

Many Spanish words became part of the American language, too, especially in the cowboy culture of the Southwest, with words like *rodeo, bonanza, bronco,* and *corral.*

While every ethnic group from Norwegians to the Chinese contributed words to the American language, Indian cultures probably had the biggest impact. When Europeans first arrived in the West, they lacked the words to name all the new plants, animals, geography, and weather phenomena they saw, and usually adopted the appropriate local Indian words. Animal words like *moose, caribou, raccoon, opossum, chipmunk,* and *skunk* are all Indian words. So are many words for plants, such as *hickory, mesquite, maize, avocado, squash,* and *papaya.* Other familiar words with Indian origins include *blizzard, hurricane, toboggan, cigar, tobacco,* and *tomato.* According to some lexographers, even the expression *okay* has an Indian derivation, coming from the Choctaw *oke,* meaning "it is so."

knit communities when they reached Oregon. Not only were these pioneers related to each other, but they were from the same town back east (or, for European immigrants, the same town back in the old country). They shared the same religious convictions, the same type of educational and religious background, and the same moral values. When additional members of these family groups migrated west, they would invariably settle in the same towns.

The groups that migrated for *utopian* reasons (to create an ideal civilization) also formed close communities, although not as automatically. The strongest tie cementing utopian communities was not family but their shared vision of a better society. Mormons literally came from all over the world to settle in Salt Lake City, and after the Civil War African-Americans from all over the East and South migrated west to start utopian Black communities (although many migrated in extended family groups).

As we'll learn in the next chapter, Indian cultures also formed strong communities, although these tended to be tribal rather than family based. Indians also kept up their close community ties even if they were nomadic and not settled in one particular location.

The Non-Communities of Mining Camps and Cattle Towns

People who migrated west with the sole intention of striking it rich and then returning home did not form true communities in the West. The mining camps, and later the logging camps and cattle towns, were made up primarily of young, single men who had left their families behind. The only ties prospectors had in common were greed and distrust. They were not interested in putting down roots and would pick up and move at a moment's notice if prospects looked better somewhere else.

Without families and community opportunities for socializing, prospectors turned to drinking, prostitution, gunfights, and gambling. The same was true for cowboys who came into the cattle towns on their annual cattle drives. Although merchants opened stores and provided services such as barbershops and blacksmiths, these camps remained lawless and structureless, and neighboring communities came to see them as a threat to their standards of respectability.

The Rise of Reformers and the Role of Religion

Most western settlers were middle-class farmers and merchants who considered the protection of family-oriented communities a priority. Citizens began forming groups that promoted social reform. Pastors of the Protestant church, in particular, considered it their Christian and patriotic duty to save the West from the "sins" of drugs, crime, gambling, drinking, and prostitution. They weren't there just to save souls, they believed; they were there to reform society.

A once busy mining town reduced to a ghost town.

Protestant women also became a powerful force in the West, organizing strong reform groups such as the Women's Christian Temperance Union in Colorado and the Industrial Christian Home for Polygamist Women in Utah. They also lobbied for better schools and school teachers and actively campaigned against prostitution.

Protestant and other Anglo-American reformers did not, however, just attack immoral behavior; they took their enthusiasm for reform a dangerous step further by associating immoral behavior with particular ethnic groups. For example, many Anglo-Americans in California came to believe that because a few Mexican-Americans were convicted of robbery and murder, all Mexican-Americans were potential robbers and violent murderers. Because

Carry Nation

Carry Amelia Moore Nation became known throughout the United States for her emotional campaign to stop the sale of alcoholic beverages. She didn't just make speeches; she pushed her way into saloons and wrecked them with a hatchet.

Carry's obsession for reform (and her family history) led many of her critics to describe her as mentally ill. Born in Kentucky, she was raised by a mother who believed she was Queen Victoria and an aunt who thought she was a weather vane. But while her methods were often outrageous, she was quite aware of the realities of nineteenth century life and did much to further the many causes she represented. While still quite young, Carry left her mother's home in Kentucky and married a young Kansas doctor who soon proved to be a violent alcoholic. Carry tried to get him to stop drinking, but without success; he died a few months later. Carry eventually remarried, but the experience left her radically opposed to alcohol.

Carry and her hatchet have become a symbol for the temperance movement in this country, but few people remember her contributions to other important causes. She established sewing circles to make clothes for the homeless and organized extensive programs to feed the poor. She opposed the use of tobacco, advocated sex education for children, and campaigned for women's rights, especially on behalf of battered wives. In many respects she was well ahead of her times.

some Chinese immigrants used opium (a drug sanctioned in Chinese culture then), reformers jumped to the conclusion that all Chinese were drug addicts.

The Chinese communities (called *huigans* and *fongs*) also developed their own reform movements, especially against the secret, criminally oriented huigans that were illegally smuggling Chinese women into the country as prostitutes. By 1880, largely though the efforts of organizations such as the Chinese Society for English Education, the Chinese Students' Alliance, and the Chinese Native Sons (organizations founded by native-born Chinese-Americans), the number of Chinese prostitutes declined by 46 percent. These secret societies were powerful in the U.S., however, and the reform movements sparked a violent series of wars among the Chinese communities in San Francisco.

Racial Divisions and Relations in the Frontier Community

Almost all European-Americans in the 1800s, even the reformers, were racially prejudiced to some degree, some more than others. The reformers believed that nonwhite people were *culturally* inferior but that they could be "reformed" and then "assimilated" into white culture. Many whites took this prejudice a step further by believing that nonwhites were *inherently* and *permanently* inferior to whites and therefore had only two choices open to them: slavery or extinction. When nonwhite groups refused to disappear or accept slave status, these white racial supremacists often became angry and threatening.

Although the reformers and racists did not agree on how nonwhite minorities should be treated, they did agree that they should be treated differently than white Americans, which is exactly what happened in the West. At the end of the Civil War, for example, African-Americans were guaranteed equality under the U.S. Constitution, yet they still faced a great deal of segregation and discrimination. Mexican-Americans were guaranteed their political rights by the treaty that ended the Mexican-American War, yet many southwestern states found an effective way of limiting these rights by allowing only English-speaking citizens to vote. It was even worse for the Chinese and Japanese, because the U.S. government denied citizenship to Asians completely. And the Indian nations, as we will learn in the next chapter, were systematically stripped of not only their political rights, but their land and cultural identity as well.

This prejudice had a tremendous economic impact on nonwhite minorities. Increasingly, the only work that was available to Asians, Indians, and

Juan Cortina, Latino Robin Hood

Hispanics hated the Texas Rangers for their violent persecution as much as the Indians did. When Juan Cortina, the thirty-five-year-old son of a prominent Tejano (Texan-Mexican) family, saw the sheriff of Brownsville, Texas, pistol-whip a Latino cowboy who worked for his mother, Cortina shot him. He then recruited sixty other riders and returned to Brownsville two months later to free all Hispanic prisoners, sack the stores of Anglo businessmen, and execute four Americans who were known to have killed Hispanics. A war resulted (the Cortina War) as the Texas Rangers tried in vain to capture Cortina and his men. As a last resort, the Rangers retaliated against all the other Hispanics in the region.

African-Americans was the lowest paid and most dangerous or physically demanding work that no one else wanted (working as unskilled laborers on railroad construction projects, for example, or as seasonal harvest workers on farms). As the country became more industrialized, many were forced to move with their families to larger cities for the work in factory sweat shops that no one else wanted. Here they were forced to live in filthy slums while even their children worked fourteen to sixteen hours a day so the family could survive. The slums became an economic trap with no way out, yet the white supremacists would point to those miserable living conditions as proof of racial inferiority.

The Role of Women in the Frontier Community

Women also faced discrimination in the 1800s. Public attitude toward a woman depended on her ethnic background and social status. White wives and daughters were relatively safe on the streets of any western town. Any man who harassed or attacked a white woman who was not a known prostitute was almost always immediately lynched. Prostitutes and nonwhite minority women, however, did not enjoy this protection and were often physically attacked by men on the street. White soldiers often raped Indian women in their attempts to put down so-called Indian uprisings, and rape was a common tactic used by racist vigilante groups to harass Chinese and Indian minorities.

Annie Oakley, markswoman.

Women also faced discrimination within their families. Frontier wives and daughters were tough, resourceful, and independent, and they often took on the physical labor usually assigned to men. Although men and women had defined roles on the frontier, sometimes those roles were changed just by the sheer amount of what had to be done. Usually men and older boys worked the fields and took care of the livestock, while the women and younger children looked after the family garden, the chickens and pigs, and all of the domestic chores such as laundry, cooking, cleaning, and mending. Because no one had indoor plumbing or running water, women did a lot of carrying and fetching. When necessary, frontier women also helped with the plowing, planting, and harvesting.

In minority communities, the role of women began to change for economic reasons. Among Mexican-Americans, for example, the men were forced to take unskilled, seasonal jobs digging ditches and harvesting crops, work

that forced them to leave their families for a large part of every year
and migrate to areas where work was available. As a result, women
took over the major responsibilities of taking care of their homesteads, planting and harvesting crops, and raising the children alone.
They also took over the more important social and political roles in
their communities. As economic conditions for minorities worsened,
the death rate for Hispanic men rose to a rate almost double that of
Hispanic women, and more and more women were forced to enter the
labor force themselves, as harvest workers, cannery workers, and
domestic workers for upper-middle-class white households. Similar
patterns developed in African-American communities.

Although white women enjoyed higher social and economic
status than minority women, even they were still considered second-
class citizens. While they were protected from public violence, there
was no protection against domestic abuse at the hands of their
husbands or fathers. In addition to stronger marital rights, western
women also wanted the right to vote, and they began to organize
women's rights movements to lobby for these rights. Through the
efforts of suffragettes like Abigail Scott Duniway and Caroline
Nichols Churchill, many western states gave women the right to vote
long before the U.S. Constitution was officially amended in 1920.
Women were voting in the territory of Wyoming, for example, as early
as 1869, and in Utah, Colorado, and Idaho well before the turn of the
century.

Children, Teachers, and Public Education

Migrants heading west on the Oregon Trail reportedly had with them
an average of 3.4 children, and about 22 percent of the women were
pregnant during the journey. While children in frontier communities
were expected to do many of the domestic chores involved with
running a homestead, they also had time for social pastimes, such as
spelling bees, hayrides, taffy pulls, and ice cream socials. They
invented competitive, physical games like hopscotch, farmer in the
dell, and tag and played games imitating doctors, cowboys, Indians,
and soldiers.

Although baseball and softball were becoming popular in the East, kids
out west seldom had enough players for a full team or the luxury of a standard
playing field. Instead, they used their bats, balls, and gloves for games like flies
and grounders, work-up, and stickball, often inventing their own rules. They
also played a form of basketball that used only one basket and involved
complicated spelling and arithmetic contests. Other popular games included
checkers and tiddlywinks.

For most frontier children, school meant a one-room schoolhouse in
which a single school master or schoolmarm taught grades one through eight
at the same time. Before the 1850s, school teachers were mostly men whose
main qualification was that they knew Latin or Greek. They were poorly paid

and generally not very respected in the community. It was common for the students (who were called scholars) to harass their teachers and to play elaborate practical jokes on them. It was also standard procedure for the teacher to administer physical discipline to the students.

After gold was discovered in California in 1849, most of the male teachers quit teaching and took off to prospect. Communities all over the West started advertising in eastern newspapers for women teachers, offering special inducements and higher salaries. The problem was that women teachers usually didn't teach for more than a few years before they would quit to get married and raise their own families, so there was always a demand for more teachers. The woman school teacher of the 1800s became a western stereotype: an old maid at the age of twenty-three, she was unsmiling, rigid, and careful of her reputation and had a name like Grace, Prudence, or Charity.

Medicine in the West

Most physicians on the frontier were self-taught amateurs who barely knew how to set a broken bone or extract a bullet. When it came to surgery or treating contagious diseases, they relied on guesswork and usually prescribed a combination of purging, vomiting, and bleeding as the primary treatment. Their prescriptions were often painful. In an age when almost everyone rode horseback, hemorrhoids were a common affliction, but anyone unlucky enough to consult a frontier doctor about the condition could be in for a painful remedy. Some doctors were known to have prescribed turpentine, buffalo fat, and even laxatives. Their remedies for snakebite included a mixture of gunpowder and vinegar, tobacco juice, bark from a black oak tree, and when all else failed, lots of whiskey. Some physicians prescribed the same treatment regardless of the patient's symptoms: remove at least a cup of the patient's blood (unless they diagnosed smallpox, in which case they prescribed doses of brown sugar).

Many settlers therefore chose to follow the ethnic folk cures handed down through generations. Although many of these were old folk medicines with little effect, some were rooted in common sense and in most cases worked better than consulting a physician.

The practice of medicine reached an all-time low during the Civil War and the Indian conflicts. Surgeons were thought to be so inept and unknowledgeable that many believed they killed more wounded soldiers than they helped.

Frontier Socializing

Life on the frontier meant long hours of backbreaking work, under conditions that were often harsh and even dangerous. Most settlers were already used to backbreaking farm work before they came West. What was hardest for many of them to endure was the loneliness and isolation. They enjoyed socializing and even turned work projects into excuses for parties. When the pioneers did have time to rest and relax, the wilderness did not offer much in the way of amusing pastimes, so they had to invent their own.

One of their best inventions was the Tall Tale. Miners, trappers, homesteaders, and traders all tried to outdo each other inventing outrageous stories and passing them off as the truth. Each group developed its own fantastic heroes, passing along existing stories and inventing even wilder new ones. Many stories were also told about unbelievable weather events — like the blizzard that produced sixty feet of snow or the winter it was so cold that the words of two cowboys swearing at each other stayed frozen in the air for two weeks. (Travelers passing the same point just as a thaw came through were scared out of their wits by sudden outbursts of profanity coming out of nowhere.) Other tales described wondrous hunting feats or fantastic crops — like Nebraska turnips that grew so large that they were hollowed out and used as railroad depots.

The pioneers turned any event into an excuse for socializing, even work. Groups of neighbors regularly got together for quilting bees, apple peelings, corn shuckings, log rollings, house-raisings, rabbit drives, and even wheat threshings. When new settlers moved into the area, neighbors would traditionally throw a "pound party" with everyone bringing a pound of some food or commodity that would help the new family set up housekeeping.

In addition to hunting and fishing, settlers (mostly men) engaged in turkey shoots, bear-baiting, cock fights, dog fights, and a sport called gander-pulling. Popular with both men and women, young and old, was lively dancing to fiddle music.

Immigrant Farmers — the Unsung Heroes

One thing almost all settlers had in common, regardless of their ethnic heritage, gender, or profession, was their willingness to take on the backbreaking work of starting a new life on the harsh frontier. Those that came to farm

A sod home and family in Kansas.

faced the biggest challenge of all. More than 60 percent of frontier farmers brought their plows and harrows and ox teams with them on the overland trail.

When they reached their destinations, they continued to live in their wagons while they built their first homes. If timber wasn't available, they carved out holes in hillsides and then walled up the open side with squares of sod they dug out of the ground. Because of the "soddies" they built, these pioneers became known as sodbusters. Their homes were crude, leaky, and

Frontier woman gathering buffalo chips for fuel.

uncomfortable, but better then sleeping in the open. Later, many built freestanding homes out of the same material because the tangle of roots in the sod made the walls strong and dense once the dirt dried. Whether the house was made of timber or sod its most expensive part was the windows. Those had to be imported from the East and cost about $1.25 a window, which was a lot of money in the 1840s.

Sod was also used as fuel to heat the settlers' homes, and it was the woman's job to make sure there was always enough on hand. Buffalo chips (dung) were also a cheap and plentiful fuel that women collected for heating and cooking. As soon as the new settlers built some sort of shelter, they prepared the ground for planting, which meant clearing timber, plowing fields, and breaking sod every day from dawn until twilight until their first crops were planted.

How Settlers Affected the Land

Settlers brought the corn, wheat, and other seeds they needed with them, but they did not bring the respect Europeans had always had for farmland. In Europe, land was scarce and farmers took care of it so it would continue to produce the highest possible crop yields. In the American West of the mid-1800s, no thought was given to planting what was most suitable to the soil in a particular area. Land was so plentiful that when settlers wore out the soil in one place, they simply moved on to another, without any regard to replanting either timber or other vegetation to keep the soil from eroding. Many forests that were not cut down were accidently burned through widespread forest fires. Everyone believed the West's resources were inexhaustible.

Mining also had a lasting physical impact on the environment. The first wave of prospectors quickly snapped up whatever gold, silver, and other precious metals that were strewn about riverbeds in nugget form. After that, the only fortunes to be made were by the mining companies that moved in and stripped the land with their heavy hydraulic machinery. These companies changed the ecology of much of the landscape by reducing mountains to heaps of slag and rubble and by rerouting rivers, which caused excessive erosion in some areas and turned rich farmland into desert in others. It was not until 1884 that California began to recognize the potential long-term effects of hydraulic mining and made it illegal, but only after hundreds of thousands of once-fertile farmlands were washed away.

Railroad construction added to this negative impact on the environment by blasting through mountains, while steam locomotives belched up smoke and cinders. In urban areas, the factories created after the industrial revolution were already polluting both air and water.

But however catastrophic the settlers' effect was on the land, their effect on wildlife was nothing less than wasteful, pointless slaughter. Species like the passenger pigeon became extinct, while others such as the buffalo and beaver came dangerously close to extinction. As we will see in the next chapter, the impact this had on Indian tribes who depended on hunting to survive was devastating. Where literally millions of buffalo had once thundered across the plains, ranchers were now grazing their cattle.

Law and Order in the West

The West was not the violent and lawless frontier depicted in books and movies, but it did have its share of people who refused to abide by its rules, particularly in mining camps and cattle towns. Property rights were hard to enforce, liquor was plentiful, and almost everyone was armed. A certain amount of violent crime was inevitable.

Many vigilante groups were often formed in boomtown areas where formal courthouses and jails had not yet been established and where local law enforcement might consist of a single sheriff. These local vigilante groups usually cooperated with whatever law enforcement there was, leaving trial and punishment of the criminals they caught to the county or territory judges. But mob rule did take over from time to time, and the vigilantes took justice entirely into their own hands. This usually meant hanging the accused wherever they caught them.

In the 1860s, for example, when prospectors began overrunning the new gold strikes in Montana, crime became so bad that local citizens banded together to take the law into their own hands. Led by Deputy Marshal John X. Biedler, the Montana Vigilantes caught scores of desperadoes and hanged them from "hanging trees." One of the most treacherous bands of criminals they captured was a gang of road agents led by a sheriff known for his corruption and cruelty.

Many of the non-Indian communities in the West depended on the raising, transporting, and processing of cattle for their economy. Cattle stealing, or rustling, was thus considered a crime of major proportions, and the punishment for cattle rustling was often swift and severe. Community outrage toward cattle rustlers often led to acts of vigilantism that could be as difficult to control as the rustling itself. In 1889, for example, when stealing cattle reached its peak in Johnson County, Wyoming, a group of the largest cattle ranchers formed the Wyoming Stock Growers' Association and hired professional gunmen from as far away as Texas to scour Wyoming for cattle thieves. The gunmen, known as the Regulators, were given a "hit list" of seventy suspected rustlers, many of them smaller ranchers. This outraged both local law officials and smaller ranchers, provoking a brief conflict called the Johnson County War. Law officials deputized bands of the small farmers and tried, unsuccessfully, to oust the Regulators. After several months, the Stock Growers' Association was satisfied that the rustler problem had been solved, and the Regulators were disbanded.

Even female cattle thieves paid the ultimate penalty for cattle rustling. In 1889, during the period

Belle Starr

Born Myra Belle Shirley, a native of Missouri whose family moved to Texas, Belle developed a passion for cutthroats and thieves. While still in her teens, she hung around with the James brothers and their cousin Cole Younger's daughter. Not long after that, she married a horse thief named Jim Reed and gave birth to his son. When Reed was killed, Belle took up with another gang and moved into Indian Territory, where she met and then married a handsome Cherokee bandit named Sam Starr. From their hideout, Belle organized and planned the crimes of the horse thieves, rustlers, and bootleggers that made up their gang. Although repeatedly charged, Belle only served a total of nine months in jail. She came to a bad end in 1889 when she was ambushed on a lonely road near her hideout. Her murderer's identity was never proved, but legend has it that it was her newest husband, a Creek named Jim July, who was tired of quarreling with her.

when rustling was at its peak in Johnson County, the Wyoming Stock Growers' Association attempted to stem the tide of cattle theft by lynching Ella Watson, a cattle-stealing prostitute known as Cattle Kate, and her lover, James Avrell, a local homesteader. When these and other lynchings failed to deter other thieves, the rich ranchers hired the best gunfighters in Texas to put a stop to the rustling.

Not all communities with vigilante groups really faced alarming crime waves. Sometimes crime was just an excuse for harassing unpopular minority groups. For example, the San Francisco Vigilance Committee of 1856 had an unusually large membership numbering between six thousand and eight thousand. The real motive of this primarily Protestant, Anglo-American group was not suppressing crime; it was suppressing Irish Catholic Democrats, which they ultimately succeeded in doing by running the Irish party's leaders out of town.

Calamity Jane

Women outlaws were a favorite subject of both newspapermen and writers of fiction, and the gun-slinging, tobacco-chewing pioneer woman from the Black Hills rapidly became an international legend. Born Martha Jane Burke, Calamity Jane probably got her name from the local press. Journalists were uncomfortable with outspoken women in those days and liked to blame them, when they could, for any calamities in their area. Jane, however, was said to have confronted newspaper editors who published untruths brandishing a horsewhip until they printed a retraction.

Legitimate lawmen in the American West were not the idealistic, courageous defenders of justice portrayed in the movies. In fact, many were not much different than police officers today. Most of them never fired a shot in the line of duty. They spent most of their time serving civil and criminal warrants, chasing tax evaders, putting drunks in overnight lockup, and generally just being visible to remind the community to abide by the rules. They dressed like everyone else and were paid very little. And it was not unusual for a sheriff or a marshal to supplement his income with a little criminal activity on the side.

Like today, not all detective work was carried out by public officers. When federal law enforcement officials could no longer keep up with the number of gangs successfully robbing banks and blowing up trains, private detective agencies like Pinkerton's in Denver were formed to provide armed guards and to pursue known outlaws. Shrewd agents such as the African-American detective Ferdinand Shavers had excellent credentials and were well paid for their work. (Before joining Pinkerton's, Shavers served as President Lincoln's personal bodyguard from 1861 to 1863.) The detective agency, founded by Allan Pinkerton in 1867, received widespread publicity for its successes and its unusual methods. Their persistency and use of psychological warfare caused criminals to fear Pinkerton agents. It also earned them the nickname "eye," which later gave rise to the term "private eye."

Life on the Range — the Cowboy

Perhaps the most lasting symbol of the American West — at least for Anglo-Americans — is the cowboy, the man who worked on salary and rode cattle on the open range. Popular myths and legends often glamorize cowboys as whiskey-drinking, tobacco-chewing sharpshooters who were either paragons of virtue or despicable desperadoes whose only thoughts were of murder, gambling, and women. In reality, most cowboys were rough, hard-riding loners, tough as rawhide and fearless as rattlesnakes. They were also loyal employees. Although range work was often dangerous, a cowboy's life was usually unexciting, monotonous, and lonely.

The first cowboys were the Spanish, Mexican, and Mexican-Indian *vaqueros* who roamed the Southwest in the seventeenth century, rounding up wild horses and stray longhorn cattle. They became known as much for their code of honor and upright behavior as their excellent riding, branding, and roping skills. Much of the vaquero language and tradition evolved into the culture of the American cowboy, although Texas cowhands would have been quick to deny it. A tremendous animosity developed between the vaqueros and the *gringos*, as they referred to American cowboys.

It is estimated that there were about forty thousand cowboys in the American West, and that the era of the cowboy really lasted only two decades, from 1865 to 1885. Contrary to the John Wayne or Robert Redford movie image, cowboys were not glamorous, adventurous, or even necessarily Anglo-American. Nearly one cowboy out of three was either African-American or Hispanic, and many were European immigrants who hardly spoke English. They came from almost anywhere. Many were Civil War veterans from both the North and South, or Mexicans who became Americans when the U.S. took over the Southwest.

Cowboys cooking.

Cowboys — diverse in appearance and clothing.

Others were freed African-American slaves or poor, immigrant laborers who couldn't find work in the cities back east.

The Cowboy "Uniform."   One concern all cowboys shared was how to dress — and they dressed for protection, not style. Their clothes had to be rugged enough to withstand years of riding, roping, and branding. They had to be warm without being awkward and bulky, and they had to protect the cowhand from rain, wind, sun, and dust. A cowboy generally wore cotton or wool long johns with thick cotton socks, topped by a wool shirt and pants, a wide-brimmed, high-crowned hat, and a large scarf or handkerchief knotted around the neck. (The scarf was used to protect the cowboy's nose and mouth during sandstorms — and of course, for the cowboy who turned to crime, to hide his face during robberies.) Many also wore vests over their shirts, both for added warmth and as a place to stash their Bull Durham tobacco and cigarette rolling papers.

The most important parts of the cowboy's clothing were his leather goods. The boots had to have high heels and deep arches to give him a firm grip in the stirrups and keep him from falling from his horse. He needed heavy buckskin gloves to protect his hands when he roped and branded cattle, and leather chaps or capes tied around his legs to protect him from briars, cacti, and rope burns. Most important of all was the cowboy's thirty-pound, hand-crafted leather saddle. Although cowboys rarely owned their own horses, each cowboy did own his own saddle and took great pride in its daily care.

Cowboys had a lot of superstitions, especially about their clothes. Many thought changing underwear was bad luck. They didn't often get the chance to sleep in a real bed, but when they did, they were careful not to put their hat on the bed. That was certain bad luck.

A Cowboy's Daily Routine. The cowboy's routine was far from romantic. Cattle were not easy to manage; they wandered away from the herd constantly and got themselves stuck in watering holes or tangled up in barbed wire. They were stupid enough to try to eat anything they came across, including rocks, brush, or wire. It was the cowboy's job to ride herd all day and keep the cattle out of trouble. They also had to repair holes in the endless fences, help calving cows give birth, brand the new calves with their employer's brand, tend to the ill or wounded animals, count the herd from time to time, and in the fall, drive the herd to the nearest railhead.

Although cowboys were almost always younger men, there were some women who proved that

The Masterson Brothers

The Masterson brothers (Jim, Ed, and Bat) became legendary lawmen for their work in and around the largest of the cattle towns, Dodge City, Kansas. In 1877, twenty-five-year-old Ed was appointed marshal of Dodge City, while his twenty-four-year-old brother, Bat, was made sheriff of surrounding Ford County. Four years later, their younger brother would join the Dodge City police force. Both Bat and Ed were respected, capable lawmen. But Bat had the instincts of a gunfighter, while Ed did not. In the end, that cost Ed his life. Outlaws feared Bat's expertise with a gun, while Ed's method was to talk his adversaries into submission. In 1878, Ed was fatally shot in a scuffle with a drunken cowboy and Dodge City mourned his death. Bat, on the other hand, had to be voted out of office, which he was later that same year by a dull-witted saloon-keeper who won the election on an economics platform. Bat traveled a lot after that, turning up as a gambler in some places and working briefly as town marshal in others. He wound up working in New York City as a sportswriter, while his brother Jim later moved up through the ranks to become marshal of Dodge.

The Dodge City Peace Commission, 1882. The best-known members of this group of western lawmen were Bat Masterson (back row, far right) and Wyatt Earp (front row, second from left).

cowpunching wasn't strictly a male occupation. Women who inherited a ranch from a husband or father, for example, or daughters who grew up in a ranch environment, took pride in learning riding, roping, and branding skills as well as managing the ranch itself.

After the fall roundup every year, most cowboys were laid off and then hired again in the spring. That meant they had to fend for themselves during the winter, on a salary that barely got them by. Those who turned to crime usually did so because their money didn't last until spring and they were desperate for food and shelter. Those cowboys who kept their jobs all year didn't have it much better. They usually ended up living in a lonesome shack miles from the main ranch and riding the fences every day to make sure they were in good repair. Either way, cowboys hated winter with its blizzards, snow blindness, cold, and even starvation. If the weather didn't kill them, loneliness might.

Cattle Trails. The great trail drives started in the late 1860s, after the Civil War. Once a year, thousands of head of cattle were driven from ranches in Texas north to rail towns in Missouri, Kansas, and Oklahoma, where they could be freighted to the hungry markets back east. In 1871 alone almost 700,000 cattle were driven northward. There were usually eight to twenty cowboys for every 2,000-3,000 head of cattle, accompanied by a cook, a wrangler, and foreman. Since they could only cover about twelve miles a day, these drives took months if trail conditions were bad.

Cattle drives only lasted until about 1895, when the railroads started laying tracks closer and closer to the Texas ranchers. Another factor in the decline of cattle drives was Kansas legislation protecting Kansas ranchers by banning drives of Texas cattle over Kansas land. Also, many eastern cattle investors pulled out after the killer winter of 1886-87 — another factor in the decline of huge cattle drives.

The African-American Cowboy. It's estimated that as many as five thousand African-Americans worked as cowboys, and in some camps as many as one-fourth of all the hands were Black. Some were ex-slaves freed in Texas and Arkansas by the Civil War, while others were freemen who came from eastern states where work was scarce. Like their white counterparts, many came just for the adventure.

In many ways, African-Americans who became cowboys faced much less discrimination after the Civil War than those who chose other professions. The tasks cow-

The Wild Bunch, train robbers, in a formal photo taken in Fort Worth, Texas, in 1901. Standing (left-right): Bill Carver, Harvey Logan. Seated (left-right): Harry Long-baugh ("Sundance Kid"), Ben Kilpatrick, Robert Leroy Parker ("Butch Cassidy").

Butch Cassidy and the Sundance Kid

Born into a devoutly religious family in Beaver, Utah, in 1866, Robert Leroy Parker (who later changed his name to "Butch Cassidy") learned the finer points of cattle rustling and horse theft by hanging around gangs as a teenager. At the age of thirty, Cassidy formed his own successful gang of horse thieves and bank robbers that the local press dubbed the Wild Bunch. Although Cassidy himself detested needless violence, the methods his gang used, especially in exploding the trains they robbed, earned them their name. Eventually, the Union Pacific Railroad offered a substantial price on his head, and since lawmen from all over the country were hot on his trail, Cassidy decided to move his operation to South America. In 1901, he set sail from New York for Argentina with a trusted friend, Harry "Sundance Kid" Longbaugh and Harry's girlfriend, Etta Place. For the next decade, the three of them robbed banks and trains all across South America. Exactly what happened to them after that is still a mystery.

boys performed were difficult and often dangerous, and those who performed them well won the admiration of their peers regardless of their skin color. Black cowboys earned the same wages as white cowboys, shared the same food, and slept in the same bunkhouses.

They did not, however, share the same opportunities for advancement. Only a few African-American cowboys eventually became foremen or trail bosses. Fewer still became ranch owners. A Black cowboy named Bill Pickett was one of the exceptions when he took the money he had won in rodeo competitions over the years and invested it in a ranch of his own. Many who got too old for cow punching became camp cooks without any cut in salary.

Cowboys as Entertainers. To overcome the daily monotony and boredom of living on the range, cowboys organized informal riding, shooting, and roping competitions. At first, these were just for the amusement of the cowboys themselves. By the end of the century, however, these events became a cash business with annual rodeos and traveling "Wild West" shows.

Nat Love, African-American cowboy who claimed to have won the name "Deadwood Dick" by virtue of his roping talent.

An honored ex-Army scout played a large part in making this type of entertainment popular. In the late 1880s, William Cody (a.k.a. Buffalo Bill) who was an expert rider and marksman himself, organized a traveling Wild West show that employed real cowboys and Indians to show what the West had been like in its heyday. Buffalo Bill's Wild West Show traveled extensively throughout the U.S. and in Europe, where many people gave it rave reviews. But this and the other Wild West shows that followed did not represent the true West. It reinforced unfortunate stereotypes that later spread to literature, movies, radio, music, rodeos, and finally even to television. Cody hired Indians to chase covered wagons, do war dances in full feathers and war paint, and then sign autographs at a time when Indians throughout the country were being forcibly stripped of their heritage and traditions. Worse yet are the accusations that he paid these Indians very little and treated them badly.

Perhaps just as sad were the legendary outlaws like Frank James and Cole Younger. By 1900, professional outlaws (especially in gangs) could no longer make a living in the West because of increased security. Some found they could only make a living exhibiting themselves with the traveling Wild West shows that charged the public to hear about their exploits.

Black Hawk, Sauk leader of the Black Hawk War (1832).

CHAPTER FIVE

Indians Lose Their Sacred Lands

For a young United States, the "opening" of the West was an era of excitement, courage, and growth. The hardships of the overland trail put European-American character to the test. As frontier life became the favorite subject of European as well as American writers, the myth of the heroic pioneer continued to grow. Newspapers back east were filled with the colorful legends of fur traders, wild Indians, mountain men, steamboat pilots, cowboys, missionaries, and homesteaders. Whether a news report or an adventure novel, the focus of almost all these stories was the value pioneers placed on their personal freedom.

The Other Side of the Story

The opening of the West was not, however, an era of excitement, courage, and growth for the American Indian. Pioneer violence and greed robbed Indians of their land, destroyed their culture, and came brutally close to exterminating them. Few writers told the story from the Indian point of view. Eastern reporters had little interest in interviewing warriors or chiefs, and no one acknowledged that the settlers who so valued their personal freedom didn't think twice about denying it to anyone else who stood in their way.

The White Man's Lust for Land Leads to Indian Tragedy

From the time Europeans first explored and settled North America, their attitudes about the land struck American Indians as strange. Indians watched the white men cut down forests, overcultivate the ground, kill great quantities of game for reasons other than food, and strip the land of its natural resources. When these settlers wore out the land and killed all the game, they simply moved to new land and started over. They gave no thought to preserving or replenishing the earth's resources. Indians also had a hard time understanding why white men needed to measure, divide, and own everything, and why they never seemed satisfied with what they already had.

Indians, on the other hand, believed the land on which they hunted and farmed could not be owned by any individual but was sacred to the whole tribe. They believed that the spirits who guided them lived in the earth and were part of each rock, tree, and stream. Indians saw themselves as the earth's custodians, or keepers, and they took that responsibility seriously.

In spite of their cultural differences, Indians believed at first that they could live peacefully with the colonists. But as soon as boatloads of additional settlers landed, the colony would need more land and would push the Indians further from the East Coast. When the Indians tried to defend their hunting grounds, the settlers would retaliate and war would break out. These hostilities continued, in one form or another, for four hundred years and fall into the following three major time periods:

Indians vs. Spanish (1492-1692). The first period covers the Spanish-Indian rivalry in the Southwest, Florida, and California from the time of Columbus to about 1692 (see Chapter One). The Spanish conquered and ruled the Indians in their colonies. They looted and burned Indian villages, kidnapped hundreds of men, women, and children and shipped them back to Europe as slaves, and brutally tortured and killed any villagers who resisted.

Indians vs. French, Dutch, and English (1620-1812). In the second period, French, English, and Dutch colonists fought with Indians living east of the Mississippi. This started with the first settlements in Massachusetts and Virginia and lasted through the War of 1812 (sometimes called the Second War of Independence). These colonists were a bit more subtle than the Spanish in dealing with local Indians — but only until they met with resistance.

Indians in eastern North America often helped new settlers by showing them where to hunt local game and how to plant and harvest unfamiliar crops like corn and tobacco. The colonists went out of their way to develop friendly trade relations with local Indian tribes, seeking them out as allies against rival European powers. Some tribes sided with the British against the French; others sided with the French against the Dutch, the British, or the Spanish. Because the Indians wanted European trade and protection, few tribes felt they could remain neutral.

First deed to Indian land

When the Pilgrims first settled in Plymouth, Massachusetts, in 1620, they were befriended by a Pemaquid Indian named Samoset and three Wampanoags named Massasoit, Squanto, and Hobomah. After watching the colonists for a while, the Indians decided these white men were as helpless as children in the wilderness and did what they could to help them get through their first winter. Five years later, shiploads of white people were coming ashore to join the original settlers, and the colony began to get crowded. The colonists asked Samoset for an additional twelve thousand acres. Even though he thought the request rather strange, he obliged them by putting his "X" on a document they drew up. This was the first official deed of Indian land to English colonists.

At first, colonists on the East Coast (especially the Dutch and English) flattered local Indian chiefs by crowning them as kings and paying court to their daughters. Only then would they ask for the land they wanted, sometimes offering a few trinkets in trade. The chief, of course, believed that land came from the Great Spirit and was not his to give, but to humor the strangers and to be polite, he would accept their trinkets and

Europeans present a treaty to Indians at Fort Amsterdam

transfer the land. This transfer often involved a special ceremony in which the chief, who was unable to read or write, made his mark on a piece of European paper. (When the Dutch landed in New York harbor, Peter Minuit "bought" the entire island of Manhattan from the local Indians for sixty guilders worth of fishhooks and glass beads.)

The great numbers of English colonists who followed didn't bother with ceremony and simply pushed the Indians off the land they wanted. If the Indians resisted and tried to drive the English back to the sea, the colonists would retaliate with their muskets. Indians who weren't killed were taken as slaves. Often the colonists would burn whole villages to the ground and massacre women and children to punish the Indians who had put up a fight. Tribes such as the Wampanoag and Narragansett were virtually exterminated by the British long before the American Revolution.

This pattern continued for two more centuries. As settlers from the original thirteen colonies moved inland over the Alleghenies and settled along the Mississippi and Missouri rivers, many eastern tribes fought hard to keep their land but lost. Many eastern tribes had fought in the Revolutionary War and the War of 1812 as allies of the British, a fact that continued to anger colonists long after the U.S. had gained its independence. In August 1779, American troops led by George Washington burned forty Iroquois towns to the ground in a massive "scorched earth" campaign. With good reason, tribes in the Northeast started calling Washington "the Town Destroyer." Before the U.S. gained its independence, these Indians had been fighting colonists for their political independence. Now they were fighting for their very lives.

Indians vs. United States of America (1790-1890). This period actually overlaps the previous one and starts with a series of wars in the 1790s. As you will read in the discussion that follows, it ends, tragically, one hundred years later with the Indian massacre at Wounded Knee, South Dakota.

Two Centuries of Broken Treaties

Drafting written treaties with the U.S. government was not a practice Indians were comfortable with, even though they had been signing such treaties since the first Europeans landed in North America. When Spain, France, Holland, and England were competing with each other for trading rights, they often drew up written treaties with local tribes to give themselves favored trade status and to gain the Indians as allies. While some treaties with the U.S. government started out the same way, many were soon being written to manipulate or actually trick Indians into handing over their land.

The newly formed United States negotiated its first Indian treaty with the Delaware Indians during the Revolutionary War. The U.S. promised the Delaware statehood (if they should ever want it) in return for helping the U.S. resist the English. Not only did the Delaware never achieve statehood, but over the next century they were forced to sign eighteen more treaties that eventually drove them from their land entirely.

The new government of the United States continued to make promises. In the Northwest Ordinance of 1787, Congress announced its official policy for governing U.S. holdings west of the Appalachians. It promised that "utmost good faith shall always be observed towards the Indians; their land and property shall never be taken from them without their consent." In spite of this declaration, good faith was usually missing in treaties made after 1800.

In 1789 the government created the United States War Department, in part to handle all future Indian matters. Until a separate Bureau of Indian Affairs was created in 1824, all Indian issues were considered strictly military problems and opposing American Indians became official government policy.

The Policy of Removal

The U.S. government figured it had four options when it came to deciding on an overall Indian policy. It could exterminate them, it could isolate and "protect" each Indian village from the towns growing around them, it could assimilate Indians into white American culture, or it could transplant them to a tract of wilderness on the other side of the Mississippi. Although President Jefferson went on record as saying the only moral policy would be assimilation, even he eventually changed his position and stated that Indians would be safer if they were moved. When the U.S. bought the Louisiana territory from the French in 1803, a permanent "Indian Territory" west of the Mississippi became official.

Between 1800 and 1812 the governor of the Indiana Territory, William Henry Harrison (whose dealings with the Indians would later get him elected as the ninth U.S. president) signed fifteen Indian treaties that gave the U.S. all of what is today Indiana and Illinois, along with

Indians moving with a travois, a type of cart pulled along between two poles.

sizable chunks of Michigan, Wisconsin, and Ohio. What the Indians received for this land amounted to less than a penny an acre.

Over the next fifty years, over 100,000 Indians from twenty-eight tribes were forced to resettle west of the Mississippi. Further west, Congress ratified another fifty-two treaties that gave the U.S. 157 million acres of Indian land in what is today Idaho, Oregon, and Washington State. The last of the 374 treaties the U.S. signed with American Indians was drawn up in 1868 and forced the Nez Percé Indians in Oregon to give up their sacred land because white settlers had discovered gold on it. As these waves of displaced Indians headed for the Indian Territory set aside for them, fighting broke out between tribes over shrinking food supplies.

Needless to say, Indians became outraged as they were tricked or forced into giving up more and more of their land through meaningless treaties. Government officials openly bragged that they did whatever it took to get their treaties signed. It was common practice to lie about the wording, to neglect to explain the future ramifications of the agreement, or never mention that the only payments the Indians would receive for their sacred tribal lands were the flashy gifts the emissaries brought to flatter their chief. It was also common practice for government officials to bribe or threaten individual Indians, to falsify tribal records, or even to rush a willing handful of tribesmen into signing an agreement even though they were not authorized to speak or sign for their entire tribe.

Almost all of these documents made promises with *in perpetuity* clauses that were never kept. Tribes that were relocated were guaranteed they would never have to give up their land again. They were also promised government food, clothing, and protection "in perpetuity," which means forever. They didn't have to wait long to learn that as soon as the treaty outlasted its usefulness, the government would break it. The Potawatomi and Chippewa tribes set the record with forty-two successive treaties — each of which was supposed to last "forever."

Removal of the Five Civilized Tribes of the Southeast. The five most powerful tribes in the southeast — the Cherokee, Choctaw, Chickasaw, Creek, and Seminole — had taken it upon themselves to assimilate into white culture. Often called the Five Civilized Tribes of the Southeast, they drafted laws, elected constitutional governments, set up missionary schools for their children, and instituted the most modern farming methods. Many went so far in copying white culture that they bought and kept Black slaves. In spite of these efforts at "civilization," southern states began demanding that the federal government remove these tribes further west to territories in Nebraska, Kansas, and Oklahoma.

Any chances these tribes had of escaping this fate were lost when Andrew Jackson was inaugurated in 1829. It was well known that he opposed Indian rights, and after he was elected he publicly refused to honor federal treaty obligations that protected these southern tribes from removal. In the spring of 1830 he pushed his Indian Removal Act through Congress, an act that gave him the power and the money to move whichever tribes he wanted.

Right of Discovery

Europeans had an interesting way of justifying what they believed was their right to land. They claimed the *Right of Discovery,* a concept invented in Spain in the sixteenth century when explorers claimed vast territories in the name of the monarch (or the commercial interest) who paid for their trip. The U.S. government also used it when it claimed certain western territories. Right of Discovery meant that anyone who discovered a territory had the sole right to claim ownership of it — any white man, that is. The fact that Indians had been living on the land for thousands of years before Europeans "discovered" it apparently made no difference.

Seminole children holding a chicken.

When the State of Georgia tried to remove the Cherokee in 1831, the Cherokee took the issue all the way to the U.S. Supreme Court. Although Chief Justice Marshall sided with the Cherokee and pledged that they could not be removed, both President Jackson and the State of Georgia conspired to move them anyway by coercing a small group of Cherokee to sign the illegal Treaty of New Echota. It became clear that America's white culture did not feel there was room for independent, peacefully assimilated Indians to share the same land.

The Trail of Tears. The Choctaw were the first of the Five Civilized Tribes to make the long journey to Indian Territory in 1831. They were forced to march from Mississippi to Oklahoma barefoot, starving, and under guard, through blizzards and sub-zero temperatures. The Creek were next, leaving Alabama in 1836. Nearly half the Creek nation died on the march or during the first year in exile. In 1837, the Cherokee began a removal that would take them two years to complete. The losses they suffered through sickness and exposure to the severe weather were staggering. Over thirty thousand Indians died either making the journey or shortly after reaching Oklahoma. Sixty removed tribes were eventually relocated to Oklahoma, some from the Ohio Valley, some from as far west as Washington and California. All suffered profound losses of loved ones, homeland, freedom, and identity.

The Collapse of a Permanent Indian Territory and the Rise of Reservations

Originally U.S. treaties guaranteed that Oklahoma, Kansas, and Nebraska would remain a permanent Indian territory. But by the 1840s, when the U.S. had acquired Texas, California, and Oregon and settlers were heading west by the thousands, it became apparent that a permanent Indian territory was not going to work. Indians complained because migrants crossing their lands to get to Oregon and California ruined their crops. The migrants complained that the Indians continually raided their wagon trains for livestock and demanded payment for the right to cross their lands. Land speculators, gold prospectors, settlers, and timber thieves were rarely disciplined for overrunning Indian lands. When the Indians tried to defend their land, however, they were usually murdered.

Some states, like Texas and California, refused to honor treaties the U.S. government made with individual Indian tribes or to set aside land for reservations. The most extreme was the State of Texas, which adopted a

Farewell ceremony of the Choctaw women

There is a Choctaw story from the time of the removals that expresses the terrible sadness these people felt when they were forced to leave their sacred homelands in the forests of Mississippi. Just before one Choctaw community was to start its journey, the women formed a procession and silently stroked the leaves of each of the oak and elm trees surrounding their cabins as a last goodbye.

policy of exterminating or removing all Indians within its borders. In 1848, the atrocities committed by the Texas Rangers triggered another outbreak of Indian war in that state.

The U.S. tried unsuccessfully to make the Indians pay for any damages they caused the migrants and to mark off protected routes for the travelers to use. It was also starting to negotiate new treaties with the Indians to take back the territories of Kansas and Nebraska. Not only were immigrants demanding access to land in these territories; the government was looking for a transcontinental railroad route that didn't cut through hostile Indian territory.

More and more settlers began to complain that the Indians were given the best land when they actually had no rights to the land at all. So in the 1850s, many of the relocated tribes in Kansas and Nebraska found they had no choice but to give up their lands again. This time they signed treaties and were moved to reservations. These were either smaller tracts of land carved out of the old Indian Territory or separate small tracts of land set aside by the state government as protected Indian encampments.

The government assured the Indians they were being moved to protect them from harassment. What Congress really wanted, of course, was to get the Indians off the land taken up by the Permanent Indian Territory. A system of reservations was just one of two alternatives considered. Extermination was the other. The main reason Congress didn't pursue the alternative of extermination was that they believed it would be too expensive. If the Indians couldn't be exterminated, at least on reservations they could be controlled. And what better way to control them than with supervised military camps where Indians could be properly "disciplined and instructed" on how to be a part of white culture.

The reservation system was also a failure, for a num-

Texas Rangers

In 1839, the Texas legislature appropriated over one million dollars to finance citizen vigilante groups to oust the Comanche. The most notorious of these groups was the Texas Rangers. One hundred years later, Hollywood filmmakers were busy creating a movie called *The Texas Rangers*. The legend that movie created — the myth of the macho, heroic Texan — influenced almost all westerns that followed it. John Wayne patterned the characters he played after the Texans portrayed in that movie. In reality, these men traveled hundreds of miles to track down and kill Comanche and Kiowa Indians without provocation and with much treachery. Indians in Texas were already devastated by poverty. When the Rangers burned their villages to the ground, destroyed their crops, and slaughtered their horses, these Indians became enraged — and desperate. In revenge, Comanche warriors stepped up their looting attacks on migrants and settlers, but every new attack just gave the Rangers another excuse to go after Comanches.

The federal government tried to intercede, but the Rangers had the support of the Texas government and of its people. The U.S. did manage to sign a treaty with the Comanche and Kiowa in 1865 that promised them, in exchange for peace, the Texas Panhandle and a few other small pieces of Texas land. But Texas protested and insisted on a revised treaty. Two years later, the Comanche and Kiowa were forced to sign a "revised" treaty that forced them to move from Texas altogether and settle in Indian Territory. Shortly after the Indians were expelled, investors from Chicago bought up Panhandle land and formed the largest single cattle ranch in the history of the West, the XIT Ranch, which boasted an area bigger than the state of Connecticut. In spite of their expulsion, not all of the Comanche went to Indian Territory. Many remained on the buffalo plains. When buffalo hunters invaded this country in the early 1870s, these remaining Comanche Indians tried, unsuccessfully, to drive them out and save their buffalo herds.

Distributing supplies to Indians on a reservation.

ber of reasons. It took until 1854 for the federal government to persuade Texas and California to set aside land for reservations, and even when they did, few of the Indians in these states came onto them. Even in states that did provide tracts of land, the reservations were corrupt and mismanaged on both national and local levels. Conspiracies between rotten politicians and dishonest manufacturers often meant the food, clothing, and tools the Indians were guaranteed by treaty were stolen and sold for profit elsewhere. During the Civil War in the 1860s, the government cut back on Indian funds, which made a bad situation even worse. As more and more government troops were pulled off reservations to fight back east, reservations became the frequent targets of squatters, cattle rustlers, and liquor bootleggers.

Life on a reservation was pretty grim. Indians were threatened by epidemics, starvation, attacks by bands of white settlers, and alcohol addiction. But these same horrors also plagued those who chose to live outside the reservation system in small settlements on the outskirts of military forts or frontier trading posts. Stories of starving women and children being beaten for scavenging the leftover heads and entrails of butchered cattle were not uncommon. Either way, existence was brutal, violent, and depressing.

Attempts at Reservation Reform. After 1850, as news of the Indian hostilities in the West reached the East, many Americans became outraged at the treatment of Indians on reservations and demanded the system be reformed. Church groups were especially vocal about the need for change, but that change happened only gradually. While many Americans living in the West would have preferred to see Indians disappear altogether, reformers from the East struggled to rescue Indian people.

Indians were not particularly receptive to the reformers' efforts, however, mainly because their plans were to assimilate Indians into white culture by forcing them to give up their Indian traditions. Their reform policy had three components. First was the suppression of normal Indian family life, including social interaction and religion. The second part of the plan was education. Indian children were to be taught Protestant values in place of tribal values. The third part of the plan was land allotment.

The Policy of Land Allotment. Allotment meant dividing up reservation lands and parceling out small sections to individual Indian families.

Allotments were designed to break up traditional tribal land holdings by instilling in Indians the pride and responsibility of owning land. Each Indian family was granted a certain number of acres — usually 160 — as a homestead. When all the families on a reservation were allotted land, the number of acres they were given was subtracted from the total acreage of the reservation. Leftover lands were sold to the highest bidder. Allotment threatened Indians for a number of reasons. In traditional Indian society, people did not live as individuals or even as nuclear families. They lived in extended tribal communities that were their source of protection as well as spirituality. The prospect of individual families living out on their own was new and frightening. The idea of dividing up their sacred ancestral homeland went against all of their spiritual beliefs. Many Indians were also convinced (and usually rightly so) that allotment was just another scheme for breaking up their solidarity and stealing the only resource they had left — their land. In spite of Indian opposition, Congress passed the General Allotment Act by a landslide in 1887. This not only made allotment legal, it gave the government the right and the authority to impose it on the Indian population.

In the 1870s, Indians were angry at being coerced into a policy they opposed, and they became even more angry when it became obvious that this Indian policy would also be a failure. When the reservations were cut up, few Indians could afford to buy any of the surplus acres, so white

Refugees in their own land

The goal of the reservation system was to break down the tribal structure. In reality, it functioned as a series of concentration camps that starved its prisoners, both spiritually and physically. The blackest period for Indians on reservations was between the early 1870s and the 1920s. Children were taught to be ashamed of their tribal heritage, and adults were forbidden to practice any of the ceremonies sacred to their spiritual lives. Physically, hunger was the biggest reality, and many Indians died of starvation. Corruption was so widespread that the food, clothing, blankets, and tools that were delivered were often unusable. The agents who cheated them argued that Indians were just a bunch of lazy, whining, uncivilized children who deserved what they got.

Some whites who had contact with reservation life were outraged with the treatment they witnessed. An army surgeon who visited the Crow Creek reservation in South Dakota filed a report about food conditions that resulted in a number of Indian deaths from starvation. He described a large wooden vat, six feet square and six feet deep, that was connected to a steam boiler by a pipe. Managers of the reservation threw several barrels of flour into the vat, along with beef and pork heads and entrails and several buckets of beans. The resulting mass was cooked by the steam from the boiler as it passed through the pipe. When someone decided it had "cooked" long enough, the Indians were given pails and ordered to come and get it. Of those who did, many became seriously ill. Those who refused died of starvation.

Most of the whites who expressed concern over conditions on reservations were missionaries or priests. Unfortunately, their interests usually centered on converting the Indians, not feeding them.

Indians on a reservation assemble for federal inspectors.

speculators bought them up at bargain prices. Most Indian families could not survive on the small homesteads they were given and soon sold their deeds to these same speculators for ridiculously low amounts. This left them destitute, landless, and with no tribal community to back them up. They were worse off than when they had been living on the reservations.

The Long Resistance

In spite of centuries of abusive treatment at the hands of whites, over 300,000 Indians were still alive in 1865. The survivors were angry and resentful at the atrocities, the endless broken treaties, and the hopelessness of reservation life. In the 1850s, a series of violent wars broke out in the West between the Indians and the whites that would last for the next thirty years.

The fighting took place on three fronts: the Great Plains, the Southwest, and the wars of resistance waged by smaller tribes on the West Coast. The first and most violent series of wars was the confrontation of settlers on the Great Plains who wanted more land and the Indian tribes (especially the Sioux and the Comanche) who were fighting to keep the land guaranteed them by previous treaties.

The second front was fought in the Southwest. These wars were not so much disputes over territory as they were attempts by Americans to control Indian raiding. Navajo and Apache tribes regularly stole horses, cattle, and sheep from white ranchers to keep from starving and to trade for other necessary supplies.

The third type of confrontation during this period took place in the Pacific Northwest between settlers and smaller tribes such as the Cayuse and Yakima. These were mainly wars of resistance as these tribes struggled to survive and maintain their independence.

Between 1866 and 1891, the U.S. Army fought more than a thousand engagements with Indians and lists 2,571 military casualties. The Army also lists the statistic of 5,519 Indian casualties, but states that this figure is only a guess. On the Great Plains, the U.S. Army slaughtered the buffalo, the Indians' principal food supply, and at Sand Creek and elsewhere wiped out whole Indian villages.

When gold was discovered in Colorado in 1859, hoards of prospectors rushed across tribal hunting grounds south of the Platte River. The Sioux, Cheyenne, and Arapaho retaliated with a reign of terror. When the U.S. Army attempted to build forts along the route to protect the travelers, the angry Sioux, led by Chief Red Cloud, attacked the forts and forced them to evacuate. That didn't stop prospectors from pushing their way to Colorado, however, or dampen the enthusiasm of the U.S. Army, either. General William Tecumseh Sherman, Commander of U.S. Army Forces, was quoted in 1867 as saying, "The more [Indians] we can kill this year, the less will have to be killed the next war, for the more I see of these Indians, the more convinced I am that they all have to be killed or be maintained as a species of paupers."

Although the Indians on all three fronts were gradually being defeated, they did have a number of successes. One of the most famous is the battle at Little Big Horn in North Dakota, also known as Custer's Last Stand.

The Battle of Little Big Horn. When gold was found in the Black Hills in the heart of Sioux country, the Plains Indians prepared to defend their hunting grounds from a fresh onslaught of land-hungry prospectors. Led by their great chiefs Crazy Horse and Sitting Bull, two thousand Sioux and their allies braced themselves for battle at a village near the Little Big Horn. In June of 1876, General George Armstrong Custer approached the village with the six hundred men in his 7th Cavalry unit.

Believing that his men could easily take even a large group of poorly armed Indians, Custer badly underestimated the forces of Crazy Horse and Sitting Bull. He probably did not know in advance that the Indians carried rifles, not just bows and arrows, and that many even had repeating weapons. Nevertheless, Custer should have been more cautious. The Sioux and Cheyenne had waged several dramatic battles against the Army in that area just a few months before.

Custer split his command into three sections with the intention of surrounding the village. Two of the sections were immediately stopped by Indian gunfire, and several parties of Indians surrounded the third. The battle was an overwhelming victory for the Sioux and the most important victory of the entire Indian resistance. The only survivor out of Custer's entire regiment was an officer's horse. The Indians paid a high price for this victory. For the next five years the Army tried to live down this humiliating defeat by waging an all-out campaign to conquer the Sioux and Cheyenne once and for all.

Geronimo and the Southwest Resistance. About the same time the Sioux were battling Custer, an aggressive Apache chief named Geronimo was rallying Indians to his cause in the Southwest. After his forces attacked and almost captured Fort Apache, the U.S. Army launched a five-year campaign to hunt him down. At the end, Geronimo's group amounted to only sixteen warriors, twelve women, and six children. Yet against them the U.S. had deployed five thousand troops, over one-quarter of the entire U.S. Army. When they finally forced him to surrender, the Army removed Geronimo and his people to Florida, the greatest distance ever imposed on an Indian people.

The Massacre at Wounded Knee Creek. By 1890, the Indians that had once dominated North America were almost totally defeated. In the fall of 1890, the Sioux prepared themselves for one last chance to win back their land and their honor.

Geronimo

Geronimo (1829-1909) was not born with that name. It was first given to him by frightened Mexican soldiers who watched him charge through a hail of enemy fire to kill soldiers with his knife. When they saw him charging, they would superstitiously yell the Spanish name for St. Jerome — "Geronimo!"

His family name was Goyahkla, and he was born in the Gila River valley in what is today New Mexico. He grew to manhood in a part of the country where the Apache had been fighting with Spaniards and then Mexicans for over two hundred years. In 1837, the Mexican state of Chihuahua officially adopted a policy of genocide by offering a bounty on Apache scalps.

The incident that turned Geronimo from a normal Apache life of hunting and trading happened in 1850. A town in Chihuahua called Janos made a peace offer inviting the Apache to trade. While the men went into town to barter the hides and furs, the women and children camped on the outskirts. A roving platoon of Mexican troops from the nearby state of Sonora discovered the camp. They killed twenty-five of the women and children and captured sixty more whom they eventually sold into slavery. When Geronimo came back from town, he discovered the dead bodies of his mother, his young wife, and all three of his children.

For the rest of his life, Geronimo hated all Mexicans and killed them whenever he could. Shortly after discovering the bodies of his loved ones, he received his Power. He heard a voice call his name four times and then tell him that no gun or arrow would ever be able to kill him. From that day on, Geronimo believed that he could not be killed in battle, and his bravery in the face of death was based on that belief.

Suspecting an uprising, the Army sent six hundred Regulars to the Pine Ridge and Rosebud reservations in the Black Hills to subdue Indians who were illegally participating in such sacred rituals as the Ghost Dance. General Nelson Miles ordered the arrest of the two presiding chiefs, Sitting Bull and Wovoka. When his men tried to rescue him, Sitting Bull was murdered by his captors, an act that so outraged the Sioux that 350 of them left their reservation under the leadership of Big Foot to unite with the other Sioux tribes in their territory.

Indians gather for a dance before being massacred at Wounded Knee.

General Miles sent the 7th Cavalry (Custer's old regiment) out after them. The Indians gave up and allowed the troopers to lead them toward Omaha, Nebraska, where they were to be relocated. On December 28, 1890, the soldiers and Indians made camp at Wounded Knee Creek and waited for additional troops to arrive with artillery. The next morning, the 120 Sioux warriors in the party were ordered to give up their arms. Surrounded by over 500 U.S. troops, they were badly outnumbered. Nevertheless, the

Chief Crazy Horse.

Chief Sitting Bull.

proud warriors refused to give up their guns. When the soldiers searched their belongings, a hidden gun accidentally went off, shocking both the soldiers and the Indians. The exact moment and cause of the shooting is still debated.

Several Sioux warriors took their guns out from the blankets they had used to conceal them and started firing at the soldiers. Some attacked their captors with knives and clubs. The soldiers immediately withdrew, surrounded the camp and opened fire on the Indians. They didn't stop to determine if they were aiming at warriors or unarmed women and children. Within minutes 150 Indians and 25 soldiers lay dead, with another 89 wounded.

American Indian culture, with its varied art, traditions, and beliefs, survived this massacre and would outlive other abuses. But this sad and needless tragedy was the last remnant of armed Indian resistance to the U.S. government. They had been defeated.

I did not know then how much was ended. When I look back now from this high hill of my old age, I can still see the butchered women and children lying heaped and scattered all along the crooked gulch as plain as when I saw them with eyes still young. And I can see that something else died there in the bloody mud, and was buried in the blizzard. A people's dream died there. It was a beautiful dream . . . the nation's hoop is broken and scattered. There is no center any longer, and the sacred tree is dead.

— Black Elk, Oglala Sioux Holy Man and Keeper of the Sacred Pipe

1400	Over three hundred active, advanced Indian cultures in North America
1492	Columbus establishes first Spanish colony in North America
1519	Cortés begins conquest of Mexico for Spain
1528	Spaniard ex-slaver and explorer de Vaca shipwrecked off Texas coast
1540	Coronado claims Nuevo Mexico for Spain, introducing both the horse and epidemic diseases to the Southwest
1598	Spaniards begin to colonize the Southwest
1607	Jamestown settlement in Virginia founded
1614	Dutch settlement on Hudson founded
1620	Pilgrim settlement in New Plymouth founded
1682	LaSalle reaches Gulf of Mexico and claims Mississippi Valley for France
1760	Spanish establish Indian missions along California coast
1776	Declaration of Independence, proclaiming independence of thirteen founding colonies from Britain, is signed
1778	Captain James Cook lands on Vancouver Island in the Pacific Northwest and claims rich fur trade for England
1779	Washington leads campaign against Iroquois in retaliation for Indian aid to the British in the Revolutionary War
1787	In Northwest Ordinance, U.S. promises Indians their lands will never be taken from them without their consent
1789	U.S. Constitution established
1803	The Louisiana Purchase and the U.S. policy of Manifest Destiny; U.S. establishes official Indian Territory and policy of removal
1812	War between England and the U.S.; maiden voyage of first steamship on Mississippi River; Russians establish Fort Ross north of San Francisco Bay, California
1821	Mexico wins independence from Spain and opens trade with U.S.
1830	Beginning of North European immigration to the U.S.; Congress passes Indian Removal Act; founding of Mormon Church
1831	Cherokee Nation takes state of Georgia to Supreme Court to fight removal; wins, but is forced to move anyway; beginning of the Trail of Tears
1836	Texans defeated by Mexico in battle of the Alamo
1840	Overland migrations via the Oregon Trail begin
1841	Russians sell livestock and buildings of Fort Ross to Swiss adventurer named John Sutter
1844	Expansionist James Polk elected president of U.S.; Texas declares independence from Mexico; Joseph Smith, founder of Mormon Church, murdered; Mormons begin migration to Salt Lake in Utah
1845	Texas annexed by U.S.
1846	Beginning of Mexican-American War; U.S. annexes Oregon Territory after agreement with England; Texas becomes a U.S. state

1848	End of Mexican-American War; U.S. gains Mexican Territory; James Marshall discovers gold in California lumber mill; beginning of California Gold Rush of 1849; beginning of Chinese immigration to U.S.; massive migrations of Europeans (especially Germans and Irish) to U.S.
1850	Beginning of relocation of Indians to reservations; organization of expeditions to determine best transcontinental railroad route
1850	Cholera epidemic in North America
1851	Beginning of thirty years of Indian wars with U.S. government
1857	President Buchanan sends troops to suppress Mormon rebellion in Utah
1859	Gold discovered in Colorado; unsuccessful Sioux attempt to save land from gold prospectors
1860	Pony Express Company established to deliver mail in the West; beginning of Western cattle drives
1861	Outbreak of the Civil War in the U.S.
1865	End of Civil War; Lincoln assassinated; beginning of cowboy era in the American West
1868	Gold discovered in Oregon; Nez Percé Indians forced to give up Oregon land
1876	Custer's disastrous battle and defeat by Crazy Horse and Sitting Bull
1880	Beginning of immigration of Jews, Italians and Chinese to U.S.
1885	End of cowboy era in the American West
1887	Congress passes General Allotment Act to divide up reservation land
1890	Massacre at Wounded Knee Creek

GLOSSARY

allotment	policy of dividing up reservation land into 160-acre homesteads for each Indian family, meant to break up traditional Indian tribal communities
assimilation	the absorption of a minority cultural group into a main or majority cultural group; the minority group is generally expected to give up its own traditional language and culture and take on those of the majority group
conquistadors	Spaniards who explored and conquered new worlds for the glory of God (and for their own profit) in the fourteenth through the eighteenth centuries
encomendero	representative appointed by the Spanish government to govern the Pueblo villages in the Spanish colonies of the Southwest
expansionism	the policy of expanding a nation's territory or power, often at the expense of other nations
fong	a close-knit Chinese community made up of families that came to the U.S. from the same village in China
'49ers	prospectors who took part in the California Gold Rush of 1848-49
genizaros	the slave labor class in the Spanish colonies of the Southwest who were Apache or Navajo Indians; after ten years of slavery, they became freed slaves
gringo	an uncomplimentary expression used by Mexican cowboys (vaqueros) to describe U.S. cowboys
huigan	a close-knit Chinese community made up of families that came to the U.S. from the same district in China

Manifest Destiny	the policy the U.S. used in the nineteenth century to justify its territorial expansion at the expense of the country's original Indian inhabitants
mestizos	inhabitants of the Spanish colonies of the Southwest who were of mixed Indian and Spanish descent
Mormon	member of the Church of Jesus Christ of Latter Day Saints, founded in the U.S. by Joseph Smith in 1830
mulattos	inhabitants of the Spanish colonies of the Southwest who were of mixed African and Spanish descent
New France	the expanse of land stretching from the Appalachian Mountains to the Mississippi River, and from Canada to the Gulf of Mexico that LaSalle claimed for France in the late seventeenth century; the U.S. acquired this territory through the Louisiana Purchase of 1803
Nuevo Mexico	area of the southwestern U.S. that was formerly Spanish and then Mexican territory and is today the state of New Mexico
pardos	inhabitants of the Spanish colonies of the Southwest who were of mixed African, Indian, and Spanish descent
Right of Discovery	a concept Spain invented in the sixteenth century that gave any European country that discovered a new territory the exclusive right of ownership to it
soddy	a pioneer house with walls and roof made of dried blocks of sod; these were often built into the side of a hill or even in a hole in the ground
stereotype	a fixed, superficial idea of what a whole group of people thinks, acts and looks like without any consideration of the group members as individuals
utopian	a perfect society, politically, economically, and socially
vaquero	Mexican cowpunchers; the original cowboys in the Southwest
vigilantes	groups of citizens that took the law into their own hands to track down and punish criminals when they believed law enforcement officials in their area could not or would not do the job
voyageurs	French explorers and fur trappers who forged trails by canoeing the great waterways of the U.S., particularly the Mississippi and Missouri Rivers

FURTHER READING

Bennett, Lerone, Jr. *The Shaping of Black America*. Chicago: Johnson Publishing Company, Inc., 1975.

Brown, Dee. *Bury My Heart at Wounded Knee (An Indian Story of the American West)*. New York: Bantam Books, Inc., 1971.

Brown, Dee. *Wondrous Times on the Frontier*. New York: Harper Collins Publishers, 1992.

Campbell, Joseph. *Historical Atlas of World Mythology*. New York: Harper & Row, 1989.

Davis, William C. *The American Frontier: Pioneers, Settlers & Cowboys 1800-1899*. New York: Smithmark Publishers, 1992.

Durham, Philip and Jones, Everett L. *The Negro Cowboys*. New York: Dodd, Mead & Company, 1965.

Goetzman, William H. and Goetzman, William N. *The West of the Imagination*. New York: W.W. Norton, 1986.

Meltzer, Milton. *The Black Americans: A History in Their Own Words, 1619-1983*. New York: Harper & Row, 1984.

Nabokov, Peter. *Native American Testimony (A Chronicle of Indian-White Relations from Prophecy to the Present, 1492-1992)*. New York: Viking Penguin, 1991.

White, Richard. *It's Your Misfortune and None of My Own: A New History of the American West*. Norman, Oklahoma: University of Oklahoma Press, 1991.